To Betty Davenport

Here's to your healing,
health + wholeness.
Blessings + Peace —

Elaine R Ferguson

Healing,
Health and
Transformation

Healing, Health and Transformation

New Frontiers in Medicine

Elaine R. Ferguson, M.D.

LAVONNE PRESS
Chicago, Illinois

The information contained in this book is not intended to be used as a medical diagnosis or prescription for any physical or mental illness or disease. Anyone seeking medical advice should contact a qualified, licensed physician. Readers must use their own judgment, consult a holistic medical expert or their personal physician for specific applications to their individual problems. The author and publisher assume no responsibility for errors, inaccuracies, omissions or any inconsistency herein.

ISBN 1-878743-17-1

LCCN 90-060985

ATTENTION HEALTH PROFESSIONALS, GROUPS, and ASSOCIATIONS: This book is available at quantity discounts on bulk purchases for patient, educational or promotional use. For information please contact our Special Sales Department, Lavonne Press, P.O. Box 81709, Chicago, IL 60681-0709 or call (312) 288-3708.

Dedication

For my parents, Mary Lucile and James Henry Ferguson. I can never return to you in equal measure all that you have given me. I thank God daily for the precious gift of your presence in my life. Thank you for being.

Good health is more than a
body that works. It is feeling good about
yourself, dealing effectively with the people
and situations around you and growing spiritually
toward a new sense of wholeness and meaning in life.

−Anonymous

Acknowledgments

In the past, I've hastily skipped over the acknowledgments on my way to beginning a book. To me the *Acknowledgments* were nothing more than fillers. I never knew how important those faceless names were to a book's existence.

That was my perspective before I embarked on writing a book. During the process of writing this book, I came to see exactly how important the support, encouragement, enthusiasm, and input of others can be in bringing to life an idea.

Without the help of the persons listed below, this book would have never seen the light of day. They have not only been sisters and brothers of my extended family, but they have been the wells from which I drank. They have cheered me when there was doubt, invigorated me when I was tired, and always been there when I needed them. It is only because others cheered me on, insisting I could write this book, that I was able to complete my task. And for that I am indebted to them and eternally grateful for their presence in my life.

Jill Scott, Ayana Karanja, Carmen Sanchez, Donna Ippolito, Mitchell Butler, Judith Wiker, Francine Smith, Judith Citrin, Dr. Marilyn Jackson, Attorney LaRoma White, Timothy Boyd, Marveline Miles, Gloria Besbekis, Steven Toot, Dr. Robin Snead, Dr. Elaine Simpkins, and Dr. Joe Baldwin were this book's midwives. They helped give it birth. From the book's initial inception over two years ago to its completion, they were unwavering in their support. They gave me the day to day—and occasionally moment to moment—encouragement and inspiration that was vital to my ability to persevere over the months of writing this manuscript.

Old friends, including Deborah Mailey, Denise Bledsoe, Levi Adams, Attorney Linda Brandon, Arlene Saunders, Moira Collins, William Allen, Dr. Claudia Weddaburne, Attorney James M. Childs, Jr., Patricia Stanley, Dr. Patricia Watkis, Dr. Kim Arthur, Attorney Sherri Faulkner, Delphine Van Buren, Sharon Shuttlesworth, Roxanna Gordy, Leslie Honore, Betty Appleby, Kathryn Battiste, Rev. Jeremiah A. Wright, Jr., Deborah Williamson, Marion and Willie Hagood, Harold and Frances Johnson, Michael Soto, Valerie Short, Gina Carter, Almeeta Steemer, Constance Taylor, Kathy Thornton, Attorney Frank Edwards, Fred Collins, William Collins, Charles Collins, Cheryl Cousins, Diretha Lavizzo, Harriet Foucher, Harold and Milena Shine, Lisa Holden Pitt, Brett Bravo, Attorney Alfreda Kinney, Derek Hill, Mae Reed, Daniel Blanchard, Burnette Tansil, and Wardell Johnson made significant contributions with their critiques of the manuscript and enthusiasm.

My patients, too numerous to name individually, have played a significant role in terms of my professional and personal growth. I have learned so much from them, through sharing a part of their lives with me. I am truly honored and blessed to have been fortunate enough to share in their moments of triumph and despair, of pain and anguish, of healing and health.

I must thank Elizabeth Bachman who originally asked me to write a proposal for this book while

Marie Brown and Katinka Matson believed it could be published.

Marilyn and Tom Ross, and their staff at About Books, Inc., were superb. They took a completed manuscript and transformed it into a book.

There are not words to adequately express how grateful I am for having been born into my family. It is because of my parents that I dared to dream. It is because of them I have accomplished all that I have during my lifetime. They nurtured me with a precious love and support that has allowed me to maneuver through this maze called life with confidence, compassion, and concern for others. My sister and my brother-in-law, Denise and Derrick Southard, were always excited and encouraging of my endeavors. My aunts, uncles, cousins, and members of our extended family, too numerous to name, have also played a part in this project.

I must also acknowledge the role that several *little ones* have played. For me these children are constant reminders of the latent innocence, beauty, and inquisitiveness that resides within us all. My niece Courtney Southard, who calls me *Aunt E-yane* at age three, and my godson Phillipe Francois Battiste, who now as a budding young man has forgotten he also once called me *E-wayne*—when he was three. And his brothers Andre and Jean-Pierre Battiste; Brandy and Brea Williamson; Dania Sanchez; Claudia, Lisa, and Akeem Childs; Nicole, Joshua, and Diana Short; Jason Saunders and Justin Baker; Jerry and Kemara Eberhardt; Kara Lara and Mark Niemoth all make me laugh and bring joy into my life.

And last, but certainly not least, I must thank God, the Creator of all that is, for being the unyielding source of light and love in my life. I am grateful for the inspiration to do this work because there are so many longing for answers to questions that too often have been ignored. I have lived a wonderful life, one that is rich—not in terms of material accumulation—but in terms of the depths of grace and compassion I have experienced. If this work brings any light to a place where darkness prevailed, healing in the presence of disease, or hope to the face of despair, then all of the credit is God's. I am merely an instrument of His peace.

Table of Contents

Introduction

For a variety of reasons, today millions of Americans are searching for new ways to cope with disease and illness—ways to safely and effectively stimulate the body's innate capacity to heal itself and maintain health.

Many are beginning to recognize the limitations of modern medicine's exorbitantly expensive, disease-oriented approach. Often this approach merely suppresses symptoms without promoting health and healing. Our contemporary health care system focuses on curing, rather than healing. It is preoccupied with eliminating the signs and symptoms of disease and illness—not in preventing their origination.

Paralleling the search for something better is a silent and frequently unnoticed revolution within the ranks of modern medicine. During the last two centuries bold and daring scientists, anchored in scientific theory, moved beyond the confines of medicine's historically limited and fragmented scope and took the tools of their trade and research to the realm of the spirit. They used scientific methods and visionary insight to determine and document the significant role the spiritual aspect of being plays in health and disease. Because of these efforts, throughout the world an impressive collection of research findings now substantiates the validity of many ancient spiritual theories and practices.

Studies clearly and concisely delineate the dramatic impact thoughts and emotions have with many pathways in the brain. It's been proven they dramatically influence the body's susceptibility to disease. Scientists have studied and documented certain measurable aspects of the *aura* – a high velocity energy field enveloping and permeating all objects and living organisms, including the human body.

The presence of healing energies radiating from the hands of healers has been detected at many universities. The effects of these healing energies transmitted and regulated by the healer have also been documented by several research scientists. *Therapeutic touch*, a secular form of laying on of hands, is taught throughout the world to thousands of health professionals, including physicians, nurses, and psychotherapists. It is now frequently used as an adjunct to conventional therapy in progressive hospitals and medical centers. The United States government has funded studies investigating the physiological impact of therapeutic touch.

Doctors have even documented the power of prayer. Several scientifically controlled studies found prayer had a positive effect on the outcome of critically ill heart patients and children with terminal cancer.

Researchers studying *out of body* and *near death* experiences have noted striking and significant similarities in the detailed descriptions of these experiences. The efficacy of ancient healing techniques, including Chinese herbal medicine and acupuncture as well as the Hindu system of Ayurveda, have also been studied and documented at many universities.

Doctors throughout the country now prescribe meditative techniques as an important component in the treatment of hypertension and many other diseases. Yoga has been successfully used by asthma patients. One university-based hospital used visualizations to supplement the treatment of severely burned patients, significantly increasing blood flow to the areas that were visualized and speeding healing. Lincoln Hospital in the Bronx, New York has successfully treated drug addicts with acupuncture and meditation augmenting conventional drug rehabilitation. And the University of Hawaii School of Medicine found electroacupuncture helpful in inducing labor in over three-quarters of the women experiencing delayed labor. Patients taught easy meditative and stress reduction skills significantly lowered hospitalization rates while at the Mind/Body Clinic at Harvard University.

These examples suggest modern medicine is on the verge of a major shift that will lead us into the twenty-first century. We're embarking on a new medicine, one that seeks an integrative approach to life, health, and healing...rather than disease, illness, and death—one that is more inclusive, integrated, and holistic. This new wave is clearly aware of the spiritual, emotional, intellectual, and physical components of healing, health, and life. In keeping with these and other developments, the federal government continues to develop an interest in holistic approaches to medicine.

This book explores a variety of ancient and contemporary healing techniques I have successfully used over the years in my holistic medical practice. My experiences have been extensive and very rewarding. In many different ways I've learned I am a tool of God's vast healing powers. The techniques I use assist the expression of the innate healing presence that resides within all of us.

This healing force is a manifestation of God's love, the essence and substance of all form. This book is written as an offering to all who seek the abundance of life and healing. It is my hope it will be a source of inspiration, hope, and healing for everyone who reads it.

I would suggest that the whole imposing edifice of modern medicine is, like the celebrated Tower of Pisa, slightly off balance.

– Prince Charles

Chapter 1

Acknowledging the Limitations of Modern Medicine

I vividly recall struggling to remain awake one morning in the intensive care nursery during rounds with my attending physician and fellow residents. After a very difficult night on duty, I was exhausted and bleary-eyed. A handful of our premature and critically ill babies had remained unstable throughout the night and prevented me and my intern from getting one wink of sleep. I felt as if my body was about to collapse beneath the pressure of its own weight. Every muscle was seized by exhaustion, aching and screaming for rest. It seemed virtually impossible for me to remain awake during rounds, yet I had no choice. After all, that was part of being a resident—to remain in a state of partial alert.

In spite of the fact I was standing, my mind seemed to float in and out of sleep. I struggled to remain aware of the cases presented to our attending physician by the intern on call with me the night before, in case the attending physician had a question my intern couldn't answer.

In the middle of a presentation, our attending suddenly began to talk about some of the contradictions of the way we practice medicine. "Just think about the time, effort, and exorbitant money—not to mention the unnecessary suffering each child and family must experience," he commented. "Study after study shows the positive effects adequate nutrition and regular prenatal care have on the outcome of pregnancy, in terms of the survival of mothers and infants, the reduction of prematurity and other complications. Not to mention the fact that in the midst of our heroic efforts we don't take into consideration the quality of life these babies will have once they leave the hospital. Rarely, if ever do we consider the impact of the long-term complications and disabilities prematurity will have upon their lives, and their families too.

"We waste too much money on technology and allocate almost nothing for prevention. Our treatment of prematurity and many diseases is very similar to closing the barn door after the horse has escaped."

I was stunned. His words struck me like a bolt of lightning. I was simultaneously confused, angered, and insulted. And yet somehow awakened. I wanted to challenge him, but I couldn't. My mind was reeling in anger. "What does he mean, focus on prevention? Hadn't I just spent the last twenty-four hours devoting all of my energies and efforts in keeping these tiny babies alive? Hadn't I missed meals, lost sleep, compromised my personal life day in and day out? Doesn't he understand or appreciate my efforts to keep these babies alive?

Let's not even think about the seemingly endless number of other sleepless nights I'd survived, usually followed by tension-filled days caused by one emergency after another. Now he's telling us prenatal care and food are more effective than my adjustments of all the ventilators, IV's, cardiac monitors, oxygen levels, and other life-sustaining equipment we use?"

Weren't these and other sacrifices a part of my desire to help those needing help? "Why bother?" I wondered. As frustration invaded my ideals and altruistic notions of being a physician, I asked myself, "Why am I here? What is the use of being a physician? What's the use? Is this worth all of the sacrifices, frustrations, and investment I've regularly encountered for almost nine years?" Even though my reaction questioned—even denied his words, in my heart I knew there was a lot of truth to what he said; I just didn't know how much truth there was. Nor did I want to know. Now I was more frustrated than ever because I felt my work was in vain.

My mind suddenly rushed back to a lecture on preventive medicine I'd heard four years earlier in medical school. I remembered the professor saying that aside from the treatment of infectious diseases and acute and traumatic illnesses, modern medicine had made very little progress in terms of *curing* diseases. Especially the chronic, debilitating ones that afflict millions of Americans. Medicine hasn't effectively treated most diseases. The professor had explained medicine tends to focus on curing in terms of symptom suppression rather than disease resolution.

While listening to that lecture, I knew one day I'd have to find another way to practice medicine—for the sake of my patients and myself. I knew it was going to be a challenge, but in my heart I was certain I'd find another way when it was the right time.

My attending physician's words could have been applied to the way we treat all the chronic diseases that plague our society. To understand the need for a more integrative, holistic approach we must begin our discussion with the triumphs and failures of modern medicine.

The expansive technological growth and development that has occurred since World War II has dramatically altered the way medicine is practiced and health care is delivered. Because our health care system has elected to focus on curing rather than prevention, on disease instead of health, it has taken a great toll and placed demands upon our resources. Our whole economy has been adversely affected by the amount of capital devoted to health care delivery.

Because of this, modern medicine today faces its greatest challenges since the emergence of our technological approach to disease. The continuously spiralling costs have led to an uncontrollable and potentially devastating burden upon all segments of our society. Attempts to reduce costs through government intervention and self-imposed restrictions in the private sector have led to increasing regulations, professional peer review, and the birth of cost-containing payment plans. These include HMO's (health maintenance organizations), PPO's (preferred provider organizations), and IPA's (independent practice organizations). All of these organizations restrict and monitor the way doctors practice. Patients are subjected to diminishing choices in terms of their selection of doctors and restricted hospitalizations due to regulations imposed to cut costs.

There is growing dissatisfaction with restrictive health plans. Why? Because the primary focus of these plans is to reduce costs through limiting hospitalization and other health care services, rather than preventing illness and disease and improving upon the care delivered, as was intended.

Physicians are forced to practice *defensive* medicine—conducting unnecessary procedures and tests—in an extremely litigious environment. This is due to the rapidly growing number of malpractice suits and skyrocketing costs. The malpractice crisis in this nation continues to escalate. In Florida during the late 1980's it became so severe, thousands of patients were refused admission by hospitals throughout the state. Scores of pregnant women were forced to deliver their babies in other states.

The way medicine is practiced now is quite different from the way it was practiced before World War II. During today's technological revolution the emphasis on something precious and special has been lost. Prior to the war, doctors had limited access to technology. Their relationship with patients was more personal and caring. It was once the cornerstone of a medical practice that the physician was more concerned with the patient than objective findings. The doctor-patient relationship has dramatically changed over the last forty years; it barely resembles what it once was. Today's training of doctors places added emphasis on data and *objective* findings, rather than the more humanistic qualities that play such an important role in the doctor-patient relationship. Surveys show a change in the perceptions of doctors and patients. Both sides acknowledge an increasing level of suspicion and lack of trust for a variety of reasons.

These factors and others have led to an environment of increasing competition for patients in today's marketplace. They have dramatically altered the face of modern medicine. Medicine has become more business like, consequently the human aspect of the doctor-patient interaction is not as important as it once was. These developments have prompted many within and without of the medical establishment to carefully analyze various aspects of our health care system.

An Overview of the U.S. Health Care System

The level of medical technology that currently exists truly borders on the miraculous. Thirty years ago the procedures, medications, and operations that are commonplace today would be viewed as part of a good, futuristic science fiction story. Such miracles of technological accomplishments are astounding and something to be proud of in the context of scientific achievements. Today heart transplants, brain surgery, reconnecting limbs, the survival of babies weighing less than two pounds, the correction of life-threatening birth defects, test tube babies, the isolation of viruses and bacteria, and powerful drugs abound. In the United States, Americans have access to the most sophisticated and technologically advanced health care system known to exist.

But our health care system focuses on disease, the suppression and elimination of symptoms and cures, rather than on health and prevention. Because of this orientation, and in spite of its technological advances, many contradictions and shortcomings exist. They deprive the citizens of our great nation from having the lowest incidence of disease and death, in comparison to other industrialized countries. In a country with great material abundance it is ironic that we have not utilized our technology and resources adequately and appropriately. We live in a nation where millions are afflicted with chronic, debilitating and life-threatening diseases—despite treatment with sophisticated and highly specialized therapies. Conventional therapy most frequently leads to the suppression of symptoms. These diseases are rarely, if ever, healed. Over half of the Americans die from heart disease, another third from cancer—while diabetes mellitus, strokes, cirrhosis of the liver, and arthritis afflicts countless more.

Compared to our Westernized counterparts, Americans living in the richest nation in the world tend to have higher disease and death rates and a general a significantly shorter life expectancy. According to the World Health Organization (WHO), statistics show we rank an appalling seventh in the world in terms of life expectancy. In spite of our highly sophisticated, state of the art technological approach to infant mortality—our infant mortality rate is even worse. Here the United States lags behind twenty-seven other countries—including Japan, most of Northern Europe, and Malta. Today many doctors, government officials, health professionals, and laypersons are beginning to ask, "What's wrong with our health care system?" Their question is repeated with increasing frequency and a growing sense of urgency.

At the turn of the century infections in this country and throughout the rest of the world were the leading cause of death. In the United States today, diseases such as heart (coronary artery) disease, cancer, diabetes mellitus, hypertension, stroke, and cirrhosis of the liver have supplanted infections. These chronic diseases are now responsible for 80% of all deaths and an even higher percentage of total disability.

Several critics of our current system have commented the system focuses on specialization, centralization, and the use of high technology. The results of this approach have been the partially effective treatment of many illnesses. According to a report released during the 1980's by the WHO and UNICEF, "Most conventional health care systems are becoming increasingly more complex and costly, with doubtful social relevance, in conjunction with misguided efforts of the medical industry to provide services."

Today many of the major areas of health care which have historically had the greatest benefit in terms of health improvement are continuously ignored. These areas include improved sanitation, hygiene, nutrition, and lifestyle changes. Statistics obtained during the twentieth century clearly shows the dramatic improvement in life expectancy is directly linked to the advances made in sanitation, water purification, housing, nutrition, and education. Studies also show the crucial role environment plays in health. Conventional medical treatment may have only contributed marginally to the death rate reduction during the last one hundred years. An analysis of declining death rates and increasing populations in England and Wales, during the nineteenth and twentieth centuries, shows improvement in the rates happened long before any direct medical intervention.

Beginning as early as 1838 death rates due to tuberculosis began to decline, 90 years before antibiotic therapy was introduced. During the seventy year period between 1901 and 1971, there was a 73% decrease in the number of deaths, due to the declining number of people expiring from infectious diseases. The death rate was marginally affected by the introduction of antimicrobial therapy. Hygienic measures, improvement of the water supply, and sewage disposal was responsible for 20% of the reduction. With the exception of nutrition, purification of the water supply has probably had a greater impact on health than any other factor.

During the twentieth century our health care system has evolved from a sovereign self-regulated cottage industry composed of a loosely organized network of hospitals and autonomous practitioners into one that is highly specialized. Since World War II, medical technology developed at an increasingly accelerated pace. This growth was primarily due to the funding and support received from the federal government. It dramatically altered the way medicine is practiced. The post-war decades of economic expansion saw a rapid growth in American medicine; it ushered in a new era. From modest prewar beginnings, the United States built an immense medical research establishment. Hospitals were enlarged and equipped with the most scientifically advanced technologies in the world, becoming the center of a new system of sophisticated care. Currently, the medical industry is the second largest industry in the economy.

During this era science was given unprecedented recognition as a national asset. Scientific advances were viewed as the doorway to an improved and more comfortable way of life. But the promises of science to cure the incurable diseases of our time, to eradicate communicable disease, and to increase our collective life expectancy have generally fallen short. In 1949 a medical expert wrote "Penicillin and the sulfonamides, the insecticide DDT, better vaccines, and improved hygienic measures have all but conquered yellow fever, dysentery, typhus, tetanus, pneumonia, meningitis. Malaria has been controlled. Disability from venereal disease has been radically reduced by new methods of therapy. Dramatic progress in surgery has been aided by the increased availability of blood plasma for transfusions."

It is a fact modern medicine has improved our collective health status in significant and meaningful ways. Yet many of our expectations have not manifested, and probably never will. Contributions include the world-wide eradication of smallpox, a dramatic reduction in the incidence of the major childhood infectious diseases of whooping cough, diphtheria, polio, measles, mumps, and rubella—which have all caused widespread epidemics, chronic complications and death. The treatment of traumatic, surgical emergencies and the intensive care of acute medical cases has also improved tremendously.

Conventional medicine is particularly effective in the treatment of traumatic injuries induced by accidents, burns, and infectious diseases. It is marginally effective in the treatment of the chronic, degenerative diseases which are the leading causes of death in this nation. Joseph Califano—former secretary of Health, Education and Welfare during the Carter Administration—found the vast major causes of chronic disease, coronary artery disease, cancer, diabetes mellitus, and the like that plague our society can be directly related to certain lifestyle patterns. These include poor eating and work habits, cigarette smoking, alcohol and caffeine consumption, stressful lifestyles, and a lack of exercise.

Califano's findings are part of a growing number of scientific inquiries, seeking to identify factors contributing to disease development. In 1988 the Surgeon General, C. Everett Koop, M.D., released a report on the affect of diet and nutrition upon the manifestation of disease.

Within two decades, between 1950 and 1970, the size of the medical force tripled in size from 1.2 to 3.9 million. In 1950 health costs comprised 4.5% of the gross national product at $12.7 billion. Twenty years later, in 1970 the nation's health bill was $71.6 billion and 7.3% of the GNP. Since 1960 the cost of health care has risen in an unprecedented, record-breaking fashion. During the last twenty years, the annual rate of increase has frequently tripled or quadrupled current inflation rates. Also, during the interim, a tenfold increase occurred in the price of rendering medical services to the nation's citizens.

In 1988 health care cost a whopping $500 billion and accounted for over 11% of the gross national product. Comparatively speaking, our nation currently spends proportionately more for health care than any other industrialized nation spends, with questionable results. The economies of most Western nations devote less than 10% of their gross national products for health care. Yet the American public has been led to believe that more technology, more drugs, and more procedures are the key to lasting health.

The technology-oriented, scientific approach has caused an alarming increase in the cost of health care, with questionable results. In 1978 the highly respected research branch of Congress, the Office of Technology Assessment, estimated only 10% to 20% of all procedures in medical practice have been shown to be effective by controlled trial. Seymour Perry, M.D., the former Director of the National Center for Health Care Technology, stated before a Congressional subcommittee in 1984, "The experience of the National Center for Health Care Technology tends to support these findings in that approximately 40% of the 75 technologies subjected to evaluation for Medicare were found to be ineffective or without evidence of benefit."

During the 1950's, Rene Dubos suggested there are inherent limitations to technological advances that have proved invaluable in the treatment of acute illness and have helped cure or correct infectious diseases, vitamin deficiencies, and birth defects. He also notes in his writings that these advances have been unable to offset the surge of chronic diseases.

The problems created by the rising costs and short-comings of medical care and health statistics have not gone unrecognized. According to John Knowles, the late President of the Rockefeller Foundation, "People have been led to believe that national health insurance, more doctors and greater use of high cost, hospital based technologies will impart health. Unfortunately none of them will." And recently Joseph Califano stated, "By the year 2000, the only person in the U.S. who can afford to get sick will be Donald Trump!" Others have noted, especially in reference to the treatment of the terminally ill, that our entanglement with medical technology prevents us from seeing the difference between maximum care and optimum care.

Our disease-oriented health care system does not adequately treat chronic diseases because of its primary focus on the physical aspects of disease, to the exclusion of all other considerations. It typically omits any consideration of the factors psychological, emotional, environmental, and spiritual aspects play in the genesis and course of disease.

Additionally, patients expect to be treated in a certain way. Many believe symptoms should be treated with a drug or surgery. They would prefer to take a pill rather than make a significant change in comparison to changing certain behaviors that contribute to the evolution of their diseases. The medical establishment has traditionally encouraged the American public to be passive consumers—to wait for developing technologies and new drugs rather than accept the role the individual plays in the expression of health and the origination of disease.

Medicine has historically overlooked the role society plays in the genesis of disease through its encouragement and tolerance of unhealthy lifestyles and behaviors. The emphasis is on curing rather than preventing disease. Individual responsibility for maintaining health is supplanted by a dependency on doctors.

So we ask why is conventional medicine ineffective, in spite of its vast resources and technologies? What is at the root of our inability to successfully treat the diseases that plague our society? Why have patients lost trust in their doctors? Why are physicians more concerned about new technologies and less involved with the total psychological, spiritual, and physical well-being of their patients? Many experts say we need more money, more doctors, and more technology. Others disagree. They believe the focus should be shifted to preventive measures. Some feel more restrictions should be placed on the *free market*. These suggestions fail to recognize the roots of our current dilemma. They provide transient solutions to a chronic situation.

The Philosophical Origins and Contradictions of Western Medicine

The search for understanding and answers inevitably leads to the philosophical origins of Western science. Historians have tended to credit ancient Greece with giving birth to Western thought and philosophy. Many authorities now believe, due to a considerable amount of evidence, the true mother of our civilization can be traced to ancient Egypt. The Greeks were taught and educated by the Egyptians. There were striking similarities between the Egyptian and early Greek cultures in terms of their philosophies, architecture, and approach to science, art, and medicine. Many Greeks lived in Egypt and were introduced to the complex, integrative view of life. It included a global, interconnected fund of knowledge, linking all disciplines together. Many Egyptian physician/priests treated patients and taught medicine in Athens and other Greek city-states.

The underlying principle of the Egyptian system was the belief that manifestations were considered to be the creative expressions of God, unity of all elements of the universe. These were the supreme and ultimate reality. Their complex belief system was a way of life. It encompassed theology, philosophy, medicine, astronomy, science, mathematics, psychology, art architecture and other disciplines into one broad-based fund of knowledge. The Egyptians were not concerned with distinctions and separations of the disciplines. Their aim was to discover the essential nature of all things.

Egypt was the first civilization known to establish a system of health care thousands of years ago. Homer wrote in *The Odyssey*, "In medical knowledge, Egypt leaves the rest of the world behind." Physicians were trained in an all-encompassing fashion. The *House of Life* served as a medical school, library, clinic, university, temple, and seminary.

The Egyptians possessed an extensive knowledge of the body, in a manner that is strikingly similar to conventional Western medicine. They diagnosed and treated many of the diseases that are well known today, including heart disease, vitamin deficiencies, colic, and bone fractures. The Egyptians combined scientific and spiritual principles in a unique manner, treating the body, mind, and spirit. Because their approach to life and medicine was a global, all-encompassing one, all elements of being were utilized in treatment. They considered healing to be a complicated process that included physical, intellectual, emotional, and spiritual components.

Not much is written about the Egyptian spiritual approach to healing. For centuries it has been cloaked in mystery and misunderstanding. It was used as a part of the total approach to healing and health, including the use of prayer, imagery, meditation, laying on of hands, and other manipulation of universal forces. All elements of being were combined in this holistic approach.

According to the *Ebers Papyrus*—one of the few medical texts found intact during the nineteenth century—their system of physical diagnosis was based on an advanced knowledge of anatomy and physiology, paralleling contemporary Western knowledge. They performed neurosurgery, bone setting, and were aware of complicated physical changes occurring with a variety of diseases. Their treatment of diseases included the extensive use of herbal, mineral, and animal products. For example, opium poppy seeds were given to colicky babies. Opium relaxes the intestinal tract. A similar drug, paregoric—which is an opium derivative—is used today for the same reason. Onions contain a large amount of vitamin C and were commonly prescribed in the case of scurvy, a vitamin C deficiency state.

The philosophical foundation and dilemma of modern medicine's restrictive scientific approach, and Western society's world view, can be traced back to the philosophical tenets developed over two thousand years ago. The origins of our contemporary philosophy date back to the sixth century B.C. The Greek system of philosophy was heavily influenced by the Egyptian culture and world view. The Greek system, like the Egyptian model, lacked division of the various disciplines. The beginning of Western science's unique approach can be traced to the first period of Greek philosophy. During that era, Greek philosophers, like their Egyptian teachers, lacked a division of science, philosophy, mathematics, art, or religion. There was no concern for such distinctions. The aim was to discover the essential nature of all things. The beliefs of the early Greek philosophers were practically identical to the Egyptian system.

A split in this unified, organic world view began when the Eleatic developed a school of thought based on the belief that God, the divine principle, was elevated above creation—all of the lesser gods and men. This principle was first identified with the unity of the universe, but was subsequently viewed as an intelligent and personal God standing above the world and directing it. Thus began a trend of thought that ultimately led to the separation of spirit and matter. It brought about a dualistic, polarized view, which became a distinctive characteristic of Western philosophy.

Other Greek philosophers reasoned that spirit and being manifests in certain invariable substances, the blending and separation of matter, giving rise to the changes in the world. The Egyptians considered the atom to be the smallest particle of matter simultaneously possessing physical and spiritual qualities. The Greeks departed from the spiritual aspects and focused on the physical. This concept found its clear expression in the philosophy of Demoritus and Leucippus. The Greek atomists drew a clear line between spirit and matter and proposed that matter was made of several *basic building blocks*. Because spirit was separated from matter, matter was viewed as inert. A concept of indestructible universal building blocks possessing various physical properties emerged from this philosophical approach and became one of the fundamental tenants of Western thought. These building blocks were believed to be innately dead particles, devoid of any element of the spirit. The cause of their motion was not explained, but was often associated with external forces which were assumed to be of spiritual origin and fundamentally different from matter.

During the centuries that followed, this image became an essential element of Western thought, hallmarked by a dualism between mind and matter, body and soul, intuition and intellect, science and religion. The birth of modern science was preceded and accompanied by the development of a philosophical thought that led to an extreme polar formulation of a dualistic view of spirit and matter.

Rene Descartes, a seventeenth century scientist and philosopher, formulated a view of nature with a fundamental division, into two separate realms: mind and matter. The philosophy of Descartes was not only important to science, but also tremendously influenced the Western way of thinking to this time. Descartes' famous *I think, therefore, I am* allowed Westerners to identify primarily with the mind, instead of their whole being. As a result of this, most Westerners perceive themselves as isolated egos, separate from their bodies. They see themselves in a fragmented, disparate way. This materialistic philosophy promoted the belief that the body exists without a relationship with the spirit, conflicting with the theological view of man held by the church.

The Cartesian perspective believed nature was innately inferior to human life, and the primary goal of life was to conquer and control its forces. This division also allowed scientists to treat matter as dead objects, completely separated from them. The material world was considered to be a collection of different objects, assembled into a machine.

Such a mechanistic view was also held by Sir Isaac Newton, whose laws and theories became the foundation of classic physics. From the second half of the seventeenth century to the end of the nineteenth, the mechanistic Newtonian model of the universe dominated all Western scientific thought. It was paralleled by the image of a monarchial masculine God, separated from His creation. This mode of thought led to the particular form of scientific investigation that continues to this day. Koch, an eighteenth century scientist, also postulated that each disease had one identifiable cause. When anthrax was isolated as a cause of disease in cattle and the tuberculosis bacillus was identified, these findings became the guiding light of Western science for the centuries that followed.

These philosophical tenets fostered the great technological and scientific revolution of the twentieth century. The Western perspectives of life and science are unique and contradictory to the manner other cultures have perceived life and science. This dualistic approach has remained essentially uninterrupted until recent developments and findings occurred in the field of quantum physics.

The irony concerning these theories is they were never proven! Who to this date has scientifically documented any of these theories? Yet changes in these unsubstantiated perspectives continue to be met with considerable resistance, even outright rejection. One of the leading researchers in the mind-body connection, George Solomon—whose ground-breaking research was reported in several respected scientific journals during the 1960's, says he stopped working in the field not because his findings were questionable, but because no one would listen!

Examples of Therapeutic Shortcomings

We have spent trillions of dollars over the last thirty years for health care. The results are questionable. In spite of medicine being inundated with new technologies, treatment intervention frequently doesn't lead to healing or the resolution of disease. The two most glaring examples of limited success and therapeutic shortcomings of conventional approaches are the treatment of cancer and coronary artery (heart) disease—the leading causes of disease and death in our country.

During the latter half of this century, cardiovascular disease has been the leading cause of death and disease in the United States. Over forty million men and women suffer with symptoms of this disease. Each year more than one million persons die from heart attacks, strokes, hypertensive disease, and other disorders of the heart. In 1983 experts estimated that nearly $6.9 billion was spent in medical care and lost wages for this one disease alone.

Coronary artery disease occurs when cholesterol deposits slowly block the artery's opening that provides blood and oxygen to the heart muscle. This blockage can occur anywhere in the vessel, frequently causing chest pain and discomfort, known as angina. These episodes of angina can typically be reversed by medication. A heart attack occurs when the artery is completely and permanently blocked. This causes the heart muscle in the affected area to die, due to the lost blood flow.

During the 1970's, after a few years of experimental use, the coronary artery bypass was introduced to the medical world. It is a surgical procedure involving the removal of a blood vessel, usually from a leg. The vessel is subsequently connected to an area in the artery in front of and behind an area of blockage, forming a *bypass*. This newly connected vessel provides blood flow to an area that was not receiving an adequate supply. Prior to the development of this procedure, other surgical interventions were used on a small scale, with very little success or acceptance. The bypass procedure is the epitome of modern technology. Today it is the most expensive, routinely performed procedure in the U.S. This procedure uses more equipment, hospital personnel, space, and total associated revenues than any other frequently performed surgical procedure.

Bypass surgery is highly overused. Furthermore, it does not cure heart disease. A decade of studies conducted throughout the country show that with the exception of certain well defined situations, the procedure does not save lives or even prevent heart attacks! Medically treated patients without surgery enjoy parallel survival rates, in comparison to their counterparts undergoing surgery. Many experts believe, with considerable substantiation, that the operation probably has a negative effect upon our nation's health.

Since 1968 more than one million persons have undergone this operation. While initially performed only in university-based research hospitals, it quickly spread to mainstream facilities—gaining acceptance and application in spite of only marginally supportive scientific data. In 1976, 80,000 Americans had the surgery at an average cost of $12,000 per procedure; within five years the number had doubled to 160,000, costing $20,000 in 1981. In 1986, 250,000 were operated on with an average cost of $30,000.

A study conducted in 1986 by the National Institute of Health found procedures costing between $25,000 and $50,000 did not prolong life! The National Heart, Lung and Blood Institute screened 16,000 patients with persistent angina (chest pain) and severe obstruction of the heart's main artery. Eleven centers found no increase in post-surgical survival rates compared to matching non-surgically treated patients. The patients were on a par with similar employment and recreational status. Critics of the study blamed the ineptitude of the VA surgeons—in spite of the fact the percentage of patients dying in their hospitals was below the national average.

Another study by the Rand Corporation concluded that indications for 40% of all coronary bypass operations were questionable. A 1978 NIH study randomly assigned patients with unstable angina to surgery or medical therapy. This study had equivalent findings. There were no differences in the survival rates.

In 1983 a study conservatively estimated at least one-seventh of all cases could be postponed or avoided, suggesting 25,000 operations were clearly unnecessary. Life was clearly prolonged by the procedure in only 11% of the cases. Twenty percent of the patients were found to have permanent post-operative side effects. This included a 5% risk of heart attack, 2% dying, and 10% serious complications such as stroke, weakening of the heart muscle, and serious infection.

Several studies have prompted experts to conclude cost incentives exert an influence greater than clinical indication, escalating use of this procedure. A survey by Cejka and Company of St. Louis found that cardiovascular surgeons' average income in 1988 was $383,520. This is compared to $100,000 for family physicians. A Blue Shield study showed there was a 75% increase in fees between 1975 and 1978. Operation rates also vary according to geography and the patient's ability to pay. The distribution of persons receiving the procedure was inconsistent with those having the greatest need. Most bypasses were conducted by 677 surgeons, each performing an average of 137 operations per year.

In the U.S., the procedure is performed twice as often as it is in Canada and Australia, four times as often as in Western Europe—despite similar demographic conditions. Why? Doctors in Canada receive

an average of $1100 per procedure, while Western
European physicians receive a basic salary no matter
what surgery they perform.

Also, science now knows there are several factors
that contribute to the development of coronary artery
disease. These include stressful lifestyle patterns, diet,
lack of exercise, and cigarette smoking. During the
1980's the interest in the prevention of coronary artery
disease captured the attention of the American public
due to the efforts of several health organizations.
Lowering cholesterol levels—through dietary changes,
exercising, and changing certain behaviors—seems to
be on everyone's mind.

The War on Cancer

Another example of contemporary medicine's
failure to turn the tide against chronic disease can be
found in its approach to the treatment of cancer. In
1930, 120,000 Americans died from cancer. Over fifty
years later, in 1986 nearly a half million (490,000)
succumbed to the disease. Close to one million Americans contract cancer each year. Except for a handful
of varieties, the attempt to control cancer has never
come close to victory. It has, in fact, lost ground. In
1971 the Nixon administration proclaimed an all out
War on Cancer. Upon signing the National Cancer
Act, President Nixon intended to launch a massive
attack to halt the dreaded disease and to find a cure
by the time of the 1976 Bicentennial celebration. In
1983 the National Cancer Institute found, after spending $10 billion, the chance of an American getting
cancer had increased 6.3% and the overall mortality
rate had increased 4.2%. The five year survival rate
increased only one half of one percent!

From 1974 to 1983 the incidence of several cancers continued to rise: colo-rectal cancer increased 4.7%, lung cancer in men 12.6%, in women 70%, uterine cancer was up 21.4%, and melanomas (skin cancers) increased a whopping 262%. There were some decreases in a few of the less common cancers, including a reduction of leukemia by 8.3% and Hodgkin's lymphoma by 13.8%. The factors attributed to these decreases were not delineated in the study.

More so than other forms, lung cancer statistics have the greatest overall impact on cancer statistics, because the disease is occurring at epidemic proportions. Prevention is now clearly recognized as the key to reducing the alarming rates of this disease. In 1985 alone, 125,600 Americans died of lung cancer accounting for one-fourth of all cancer deaths combined. Meanwhile another 144,000 people developed it. The mortality rate within ten years increased 15.4% for men and a phenomenal 71.6% for women.

Until recently, the main thrust of cancer therapy research and that of other chronic, debilitating diseases has been to identify a cure, a *magic bullet* to eradicate the disease. Researchers are beginning to move away from the belief that a single drug or therapy can cure diseases. They are starting to acknowledge the effects of lifestyle, diet, vitamin deficiencies, emotional states, and other factors on the development of disease.

The Role of the Patient

In a study conducted by medical economist, Victor Fuchs, the health statistics of the states of Nevada and Utah were compared. These two states have nearly identical income, education, and age distributions—but strikingly different disease and death rates. Nevada residents had a statistically significant higher death rate and incidence of life threatening diseases. Fuchs determined that with the exception of severely traumatic injuries, which require immediate surgical intervention, the mortality rate of each state was determined by lifestyle patterns, not access to health care services. The residents of Utah—a state with a high percentage of Mormons—had a much healthier lifestyle in comparison to Nevada—a place known for its fast paced way of life, plus a high rate of alcohol, nicotine, and drug consumption.

All of these disorders are directly linked to certain lifestyle patterns—diet, smoking, excessive caffeine and alcohol consumption, lack of exercise, and exposure to environmental toxins. One study found lack of exercise, obesity, smoking, and excessive alcohol consumption may account for over half of the deaths in the United States.

Because of the manner contemporary medicine is fashioned, doctors are frequently placed in a position of power, creating an atmosphere that encourages dependency in which the patient is induced to acquiesce. We are not trained to tailor our therapies to the psychoemotional needs of the individual, but expect the patient to conform to our unflexing and rigid approach to diagnosis and treatment. The patient is encouraged not to make choices but to continuously accept decisions, pronouncements, therapies, invasive procedures, and surgery—which are more often than not made without taking into consideration each person's particular needs.

As mentioned earlier in this chapter, the individual plays a vital role in the creation of disease. Poor living habits, self-pollution, and drug and alcohol consumption increases the chance of developing disease. Americans spend over $10 billion on tobacco, $10.5 billion on alcohol and wine, and $35 million on stimulants and tranquilizers. Forty million people spend over $1 billion dollars trying to control their weight. Drug abuse is epidemic in our society. Many unhealthy behaviors are tolerated, reinforced, and even rewarded by our society. Overeating, overworking, and the lack of exercise are all examples.

Because of these and other limitations, today segments of our society are calling for changes in our health care system. Many are seeking an approach that includes science, but also incorporates other aspects and approaches to therapy.

A Call for Holism

Our society has evolved to view the world as a collection of disassociated parts. We often think of ourselves as constituents of a mechanical world and universe. This view has infiltrated every aspect of our external and internal reality as individuals, families, communities and a society. This schism has allowed the present inner fragmentation, which mirrors our world view. It is seen as a compendium of separate, unrelated objects and events. The natural environment is treated as if it was also composed of separate, unrelated parts that have been exploited and abused by our industrialized societies. The fragmented view is further reinforced by the notions of different nations and races as well as religious and political groups. All these fragments in ourselves and our society aren't really distinct and can be seen as the essential reason for many of our present social, ecological, and cultural crises. They have alienated us from ourselves, our families, other human beings, and nature. This world-view fosters competition rather than cooperation.

Our society has been deeply affected by medicine's limited scientific scope. The need for a more integrated, holistic, humanistic, and preventive approach to health and disease clearly emerges. It is a fact: science and humanity are inextricably linked together. We are also bound to our spiritual essence, an aspect of being that Western science has failed to recognize for centuries. Medicine is only one of the disciplines within our society which manifests the contradictions of our dualistic approach—the separation of science from spirit, mind from body, intuition from rationality, creativity from intellectualism, masculine from feminine.

Many doctors report a desire to include spiritual aspects in their practice. A growing consumer dissatisfaction with contemporary therapy has been noted. Many are seeking to reform the contemporary medical system—from a reductionistic scientific approach to one more holistically oriented, one that focuses on health and healing instead of curing and disease. The medical paradigm continues to be actively transformed as credible alternative therapies emerge. Technology and humanity are inseparable. Technology is not the problem. The way we use it is. A formidable holistic health movement carries within it the seeds of a whole new approach to national health care. The search for holism clearly complements other collective and individual efforts to bring harmony and balance to the disparate segments of our world. It is the search to incorporate the neglected spiritual aspect of our existence. As we approach the end of the twentieth century and the beginning of a new millennium, perhaps we shall see in our lifetimes the emergence of the medicine of healing.

The avenues to healing are infinite. Why? Because the body heals itself. That is a reality from which we can never escape.

—*Anonymous*

Chapter 2

The Role of Holistic Medicine

When I receive calls from prospective patients I'm frequently asked, "Dr. Ferguson, I called because I'm looking for a *holistic* doctor. I like the concept; could you tell me exactly what a *holistic* doctor does?" Or I hear, "I'm feeling very comfortable about coming to see you. I understand you combine regular medicine with ancient healing therapies."

Because a universally accepted definition of holistic medicine and holistic health doesn't exist, there is some confusion and misunderstanding about these concepts. The terms mean different things to different people. To one person holistic medicine may mean going to an acupuncturist while for another it may mean eating the proper food, exercising, and taking vitamins. And to others it means saying a prayer for healing.

Many are cultivating an interest in the holistic and spiritual aspects of healing. This is due to an increasing concern about health among the American population, as well as a growing dissatisfaction with conventional medicine's inability to effectively combat the major causes of death and disease in this country and the chronically skyrocketing costs of health care. Millions of Americans are currently investigating and using several ancient healing techniques, changing unhealthy lifestyle patterns, meditating, exercising more often, and eating more nutritious foods. People afflicted with disease are seeking therapies to complement the traditional approach to illness. They are acknowledging the roles body, mind, and spirit play in the creation of disease and the healing process.

For nearly half a century, modern medicine has been mesmerized, held captive in a technological maze. Now we are beginning to seek a way out of our current dilemma. As we approach the end of this century perhaps we shall see the emergence of a medicine of healing—one that will transform the traditional, curative approach to medicine while maintaining its finest aspects. We may experience a medical hybrid of ancient and modern techniques and approaches.

The growing interest in this field of medicine is part of a large movement in our nation. It continues to gain momentum. Today many segments of our society—including doctors, patients, other health professionals, and government officials—are beginning to call for integrative and holistic methods to treat illnesses and diseases. The sweeping changes will affect all of us and alter forever the way medicine is practiced. These changes contain a potential to have a much greater impact on medicine than the technological revolution did. The relationship between doctor and patient, therapist and client, hospital and patient—and the way our society at large views medicine and healing—will be recreated in the light of a more encompassing and compassionate understanding of our true nature.

The term *holistic medicine* serves as a reminder of the great tradition that gave birth to Western medicine. It points us toward methods endured throughout the ages in the healing arts, as we seek to regain that lost aspect of our heritage. And for our society, a synthesis of contemporary medicine and the encompassing tradition of healing, promises new hope and longer life.

Understanding Holistic Medicine

From the days of the ancient Egyptians, through the healers and physicians of the Orient, Native America, Africa, Kahuna and Native Australia, man has been viewed as a composite, complex, multi-dimensional entity composed of body, mind, and a spirit that is a direct link to all of life and its creator. The majority of the mystics, healers, and priests of various traditions have all employed techniques and therapies that take into consideration this multi-dimensional aspect.

Contemporary holistic medicine is a system of health care that emphasizes the use of natural healing abilities of the patient and taking personal responsibility. It fosters a spirit of cooperation and caring among those involved, which leads to optimal healing and health. Drawing from vast resources, it encompasses a panorama of safe modalities of diagnosis and treatment, including the use of medicine and surgery. Holistic medicine looks at the whole person and all factors that contribute to the development of disease and the creation of health. It includes evaluation and analysis of physical, nutritional, environmental, emotional, and spiritual factors. Holism fosters independence and autonomy as well as responsibility in the process of healing.

A holistic approach to health emphasizes the necessity of looking at the complete person. It recognizes the fundamental and innate capacity of the body to heal itself and the role the various aspects of being play in this process. Holistic medicine affirms and recognizes the essential nature of being is derived from the spirit, the primary source of healing. Physicians practicing holistic medicine use safe forms of diagnosis and treatment, including the use of conventional medication and surgery.

The foundation of a holistic approach to medicine for our time, as in the case of all other systems, rests in a holistic view of life in which the spirit is considered to be the source of all creation and the primary manifestation of divine love. It believes all elements of creation are inextricably linked as a part of the greater whole. And it acknowledges the role spirit plays in guiding the forces and laws of the universe. Holism holds a sacred regard for all life and views the whole as being greater than the sum of its parts.

This philosophy is quite different from our contemporary view of the world. For several centuries physicians have, with a fervor equaling that of religious zealots, adhered to the belief that the scientific, reductionistic, rational approach is the ultimate source of truth and understanding. This arrogant and myopic view has blinded us to other ways of interpretation.

First, we must appreciate the differences first between the fundamental philosophies of holism and scientific thought, before we try to understand and compare the approach and use of different therapies. Orthodox medicine has long been considered the ultimate and best form of therapy. Instead of viewing it as one among several systems of health care, it has ostentatiously considered the others in an antagonistic fashion. We are now witnessing the beginning of a shift in this view—from the rigid, mechanical perspective that has guided Western civilization for almost four hundred years—to one more global and organic in its view of life. The evolving shift in perspectives from a mechanistic to organic view of the world may be the first significant change in Western thought since Bacon and Descartes.

This movement leads us back to the holistic origins of Western medicine, which flourished over 7,000 years ago. As we move from that old philosophy, hopefully to one that is more holistic and reflective of our collective experiences and aspirations, this new world view is surprisingly supported by recent developments in the field of quantum physics. These developments show the order and interrelationships of subatomic particles.

A holistic view affords and stimulates a wider sphere of involvement—including a high level of social, ecological, and political awareness—a commitment to life and the surrounding world. The world peace movement, the ecological movement, and the holistic health movement all stem from this burgeoning view of life. These and other efforts represent a growing commitment to life and our surrounded world. It is a way of life that includes a positive approach to health and healing. As more people begin to recognize this ancient principle of unity, it will increasingly stimulate harmonious interactions and efforts that are reflective of this philosophy. One of the major thrusts of this growing holistic philosophy has been the emergence of a whole approach to health and healing. Perhaps this is the beginning of a new era of scientific understanding that will unveil the mysteries of faith, hope, and healing.

Holism recognizes the underlying spiritual nature of all creation and the role spirit plays in guiding the forces of the universe. It views creation as a manifestation of the spirit and the unifying force and source of all love. It recognizes the interconnectedness of all creation with spirit as the unifying force—unity and wholeness are the inextricable link of all creation.

A holistic view considers love as the essential underlying nature of creation and the essence of all healing. It recognizes the spiritual aspect of being, the divine essence as the source of love that manifests and guides health and healing alike. It is the spirit of love that manifests the body's inherent capacity to heal and regenerate itself physically, emotionally, and spiritually.

This approach to medicine recognizes the role all aspects of being—mind, body and spirit—play in health and disease. Holistic medicine is an integrative healing art. Holism, wholeness, healing, and holiness are all expressions and ideas springing from the same root in language and in experience.

The longer I practice, the less I am impressed by techniques. I am aware of their utility as vehicles for the healing, but I am awed by the inner healing force that we all possess. I see holistic medicine as an integral part of a philosophy and way of life, not necessarily a set of therapies. Any therapy or healing technique—a medication, a surgical procedure, a herb, for instance—all primarily stimulate the body's natural healing force.

I choose to use the term *holistic* in comparison to *alternative* or *humanistic* because it is an expansive and all-inclusive concept. Because of our dualistic, either-or perceptions, we tend to perceive that which is different as contradictory and in opposition to the standard. This is not necessarily the case. Nor does it have to be. The traditional can be complemented and expanded upon. Holistic medicine is more, much more than an *alternative* medicine. It includes the use of non-traditional therapies without necessarily perceiving a conflict. Why can't the techniques of Western medicine be merged with ancient healing ones? Holism does not perceive a conflict because it sees the body as the true source of all healing and utilizes appropriate and safe technologies and techniques. This combination creates a powerful healing arsenal.

There is an element within the holistic health movement that advocates the total abandonment of conventional medicine. I believe this is just as extreme as mainstream medicines' historical refusal to consider any other way of healing. Our resources and technology—as well as our hearts and minds—should be devoted to creating an environment that promotes health and well-being, the prevention of disease, and a medical philosophy that truly practices the art of healing. I often tell my patients if I ever get sick, I've left instructions to take me to the hospital—and have my healer meet me there!

For me holistic medicine has evolved to be much more than a group of *alternative therapies*. It is the healing tradition of a unified way of life. The same therapy may be used in many different perspectives. A doctor using *non-traditional* therapy such as acupuncture or herbs does not necessarily insure that he or she is a *holistic* doctor. Some doctors and therapists claim to be holistic when they are not. They maintain an orthodox mind-set while replacing conventional therapies with others. I've seen people claim several different techniques to be the ultimate therapeutic approach. I've heard vitamins were the answer, diet is the quintessential factor, or everything comes from the mind.

Unfortunately such attitudes supplant and extend the arrogance and limitations of the scientific approach. The body heals itself. That is a reality. A seemingly infinite source of therapies can be helpful in terms of stimulating the expression of that innate healing and restorative response.

The doctor's philosophy is the determining factor, much more so than the therapy itself. I have met many therapists who firmly believe their particular therapy is the only one that causes healing. This is sad. In reality it is a way of approaching health care—an attitude of thoughtful openness to everything that may be useful in health care, to the healthy techniques we may have ignored—that is most desirable. The things we learned in medical school and specialty training, the healing power of the therapeutic encounter, our patients capacity to understand and care for themselves, and our ability and need as physicians to grow and change—all these have bearing on the final result. As in the case of other cultures, the concept of holistic medicine is evolving and tailored to meet the specific needs of the members of our society. Healing systems are reflective of the particular beliefs and needs of a culture.

Holistic medicine moves from a cure-oriented, disease approach—one that is primarily concerned with fostering health, the prevention of disease, and the promotion of healing. It provides an opportunity to ease the heavy financial burden our health care system has placed upon our economy by using safer, less expensive methods that foster healing in a more effective manner. Also it places an emphasis on healthy lifestyles to balance our reliance on technology.

During the last twenty years there has been a significant change in attitudes concerning health and medicine. People are much more health conscious. There is a growing interest, particularly in terms of cost-effective therapies. Recently the state of California, for instance, passed a law to allow insurance companies the opportunity to pay for acupuncture and other modalities.

Because of my experience in my holistic practice, I see the great promise and potential holistic medicine offers contemporary medicine. The incorporation of spiritual techniques into modern medicine offers great possibilities for wide-scale emergence of a contemporary holistic medicine that is unique to our particular needs and resources. It offers the opportunity to overcome the philosophical and expressed shortcomings of modern medicine, to create a genuine healing art—one that could assist in the alleviation of suffering and decrease the nation's skyrocketing costs of medical care. I see waiting on the frontier of science and medicine the possibility of developing a new medicine, whose major thrust will be the creation and maintenance of health, instead of the treatment of symptoms.

Due to our rational view of the phenomenal world, for centuries the physical body has eclipsed all other aspects of being, including our psychological, emotional, intellectual, and spiritual components. In comparison, holistic medicine for our time and culture recognizes the role various dimensions of being play in the synthesis of human life. It revolves around a concept of oneness manifesting through the integration of all aspects and disciplines. Holistic medicine focuses primarily on the whole person, rather than the symptoms of a disease.

In my holistic practice I've seen a reduced need for hospitalization, decreased reliance on medication, and less frequent doctor visits among my regular patients. Other studies, including the work of Dr. Joan Borysenko of the Harvard Medical School, had similar findings. I am certain the same would apply to the population at large. A holistic medical approach can be extended to the masses. It offers an inexpensive, efficient, cost-effective, and satisfying modification of conventional practice.

Holistic medicine is a comprehensive approach to health and disease. The foundation of my practice is based on combining my years of medical education, several years of research of a wide range of therapies and ancient spiritual traditions, as well as training with African, Native American, American, and Oriental healers. Because of these experiences—and my traditional training as a physician—I believe the best and most enduring form of healing is not necessarily achieved by a single therapy, but a comprehensive and integrative approach that may employ several therapies.

In my practice every patient undergoes a detailed evaluation. It includes the medical, psychological, educational, nutritional, employment, and lifestyle history of each patient. A physical examination and appropriate diagnostic evaluation are included. We review the findings and I make extensive recommendations. They can include meditation, guided visualization, herbal preparations, dietary modifications, vitamin supplementation, acupuncture, laying on of hands, homeopathy, and others. Each patient's treatment plan takes into consideration the disease, plus his or her particular needs and beliefs. I have treated a wide variety of problems, including heart disease, cancer, hypertension, diabetes, AIDS, endometriosis, asthma, rheumatoid arthritis, burn-out, severe dermatitis, and others augmenting conventional medicine with complementary traditional healing techniques. I don't use a particular therapy for a particular disease state. Each person is afforded the opportunity to select the therapies he or she is comfortable with, based on my recommendations. Acknowledging the important role beliefs play in the healing process, I don't force patients to do anything or participate in any therapy they are not willing to accept. I also have seen that the more severe and terminal the patient's disease is, the more he or she is usually willing and open to any suggestion.

I am very much aware of the physician's position of power and how it places patients in a dependent, even infantile role. In many ways the doctor-patient relationship is similar to a parent-child relationship and fosters dependency. I believe equality should exist in this relationship. It should be a healing alliance and a therapeutic partnership, not a therapeutic autocracy.

My relationship with patients is grounded in mutual respect and concern. It promotes autonomy and independence as a part of the healing process. I do not perceive myself as an authority or healer, but as a guide and facilitator in the healing process. Holistic medicine emphasizes personal responsibility and participation during the therapeutic experience. The ultimate goal is to enable the patient to live life fully and abundantly.

From my vantage point as both a physician and a spiritual seeker, I recognize the advantages and possibilities a holistic approach to health, disease, and healing has to offer to our society. Holistic medicine emerges as an opportunity to blend the best of all worlds, using whatever is appropriate in a given situation.

A holistic approach considers any form of disease to be an important message to be dealt with consciously as a part of the life process, not as victimization by a hostile environment. Rather than focusing on the diseased portion of the body or the psyche, it employs the broader aspects of life—including nutrition, environment, intellect, lifestyle, emotional, and spiritual components—in the creation and maintenance of health and the process of healing. Because a holistic approach fosters the innate healing process, it does not recommend one therapy over another. Holistic medicine enables good health to emerge from within the individual. It fosters autonomy and independence, recognizing the stresses of life and undertaking a commitment to maintain self-expression in an environment of goodwill.

While holistic medicine emphasizes health and wellness, it also considers the process of healing of an individual as a part of a greater process involving the healing of our planet. It focuses on fostering the health of the individual in relationship to family, the society at large, the environment, and ultimately all of creation.

The most significant aspect of this concept is the idea that each one of us is responsible for his or her creation and maintenance of health. Disciplining against chronic self-abuse, evaluating our own moral and ethical standards of living, and the ultimate elimination of poverty will do much to improve the quality of life.

What is Health?

For decades health was considered to be survival long enough to reproduce. The concept of health is now evolving beyond the view that health is the absence of any detectable physical or psychological signs of disease. We don't have to be sick to be unhealthy. We can be physically intact but emotionally diseased, spiritually void.

Clearly there is a need for a broader, more encompassing definition. Health is a state of well-being and vitality where the individual is able to express his or her physical, emotional, intellectual, creative, and spiritual capacities in a manner that is harmonious with that individual, others, society, the earth, and the entirety of creation. Health is not an end, it is a process—a means that enables us to serve our life purpose, to live fully and abundantly.

Health is not achieved only treating physical symptoms, while ignoring the underlying psychological and emotional issues causing illness. To achieve a balanced state of health one must take into consideration physical, emotional, and psychological factors to develop an effective treatment plan.

The larger issue of becoming healthy revolves around the willingness to accept responsibility for healing the disease and illness and to explore those aspects which defy personal wholeness. It seems that a unique aspect of the human experience is the opportunity to weave together the many facets of one's evolving life pattern into a meaningful whole.

The management of illness requires understanding of as many of these influences as possible. Disease is a manifestation of an existing imbalance that the individual is unable to resolve on any level. It is caused and shaped by a number of influences which may or may not bear a direct causal relationship to each other.

I feel privileged and honored to have had the opportunity to witness the manifestation and expression on several occasions of the tremendous innate healing power that each of us possesses. Its presence is awesome and powerful, to the extent that descriptions are shadows of the experiences. I've seen the *miracle* of terminal cancers suddenly disappearing from bodies racked with pain and anguish. I've seen the *dead* return to life, their bodies remarkably unaffected by the death experience. And I've watched children, little premature babies too tiny to exist on their own, survive against insurmountable odds. These and other experiences have convinced me of the urgent need for transformation and change of both our philosophy and health care system. This will make these *miracles* of health and healing available to as many Americans as possible.

The Move Toward Holistic Healing

For a variety of reasons today many segments of our society, both within and out of the medical establishment, are calling for a new approach to health care—one that incorporates the best of conventional medicine with all aspects of being. Many doctors report a desire to include spiritual aspects in their practice of medicine, while a growing dissatisfaction with conventional therapy has been reported among laypersons. This is noted in the growing use of *alternative* therapies, including acupuncture, herbal therapies, biofeedback, and other nontraditional treatments. Many are seeking to reform our medical system, attempting to shift from the rational scientific approach to one that is more holistically oriented. As credible alternative therapies continue to emerge and more interest occurs, the call for change will have a greater chance of reforming itself.

During the late 1970's the American Holistic Medical Association was formed. Since its inception this organization has been at the forefront of the movement toward the mainstream acceptance of holistic medicine. Metaphysicians is a California-based organization, headed by Dr. Terrence Tyler. It was created to serve as a support network for physicians that incorporate a spiritual aspect into their practice and as a referral network for patients seeking a holistic approach to their medical problems.

Throughout our nation many holistically-oriented physicians have established centers that treat the total person. They use a global approach, one that is a science of life and healing. For example, Hunter Patch Adams, M.D., is in the process of constructing a $5 million holistic medical community, including a 40-bed hospital in Pocahontas County, West Virginia. It will be supported by donations and fund raising instead of charging patients and billing third party insurers.

According to Dr. Adams, "What I want to do is to give every healer, every health professional, the environment necessary to serve humanity unencumbered by paperwork, malpractice and the business aspect of medicine." He plans to create a hospital where mainstream scientists and doctors work side by side with psychics and homeopaths—a place where laughter and play are preventive and patients pull their own weight.

The movement has been recognized by diverse segments of the medical establishment, including the American Medical Association. Malcolm Todd, M.D., past president of the AMA stated, "Medicine has passed through its golden years. The concept of holistic medicine is gaining acceptance or at least tolerance in the medical establishment." He has vocally supported a more inclusive approach and the concept of holistic medicine.

Boston University Medical Center launched an innovative training program for physicians interested in a holistic approach to treating elderly patients. The program included training in meditation, relaxation, exercise, art, and music. It focused on the patients in the south end of Boston, one marked by excessive mortality—twice the rate of the entire state. It was successful in reducing the use of extremely costly emergency medical services, while the death rate improved.

The search for holistic medicine clearly complements other collective and individual efforts to bring harmony and balance to the seemingly disparate segments of our world. It is an attempt to incorporate the long neglected spiritual aspect of our existence into our daily lives.

Several years ago a national conference on holistic health entitled, "Healing Center of the Future," was held at the University of San Diego. Dr. Elizabeth Kubler-Ross spoke about the need for change of individual consciousness, of the inexorable power of love. She also shared her beliefs that death does not exist, based on evidence from the clinical death recoveries and the visions of dying patients.

"You should be thankful to be alive at this time of transition. We are at the beginning of a very, very difficult time, not only for this country, but the whole planet," Kubler-Ross cautioned. "Because we have lost genuine spirituality, the only thing that will bring about change into this new age is that we will be shaken. You have to know not to be afraid of that...to keep an open channel and an open mind. Learn to get in touch in silence within yourself and know that everything in this life has a purpose."

During the 1970's and 1980's our federal government made several overtures, including commissioning studies to investigate the feasibility of implementing various aspects of holistic health. A conference entitled, "Holistic Health: A Public Policy," attempted to consider the role of belief systems and alternatives in health, especially as they relate to the coming national health insurance. A variety of ancient healing techniques—including yoga, Buddhist meditative techniques, electromedicine, alternative birth approaches, therapeutic touch healing, biofeedback, imagery, and the implementation of holistic health centers—were discussed.

The conference adopted a resolution recommending action on holistic health care by the Office of Technology Assessment which serves Congress, the White House, and the Secretary of Health, Education and Welfare. Representatives of several government agencies participated in the drafting of the resolution. It emphasized the value of a holistic approach, the need to understand the principles behind its successes, and the development and evaluation of new techniques and integrated health care models.

During the conference government representatives expressed the hope that increased use of holistic and preventative approaches might ease the growing burden of medical costs. Advocates and practitioners of alternative approaches voiced concern that national health insurance, if not comprehensively organized, could lock the country into the inadequate conventional model.

If holistic medicine has provided its proponents with a rallying point, it also offers us and our critics a challenge. We need to achieve a balance between openness to unconventional healers and regulation of unscrupulous practitioners who feed off the despair of desperate patients. There is nothing holistic about allowing poorly trained personnel to practice while condemning more traditional medical care—or claiming that diet, chiropractic, acupuncture, or homeopathy can cure every illness. This is irresponsible medicine.

The doctor of the future will give no medicine, but will interest his patient in the care of the human frame, in diet and in the cause and prevention of disease.

—Thomas Edison

Chapter 3

The Transformational Journey from Physician to Healer

I am frequently asked by patients, colleagues, and friends, how I got through medical school and residency without completely accepting the orthodox approach to medicine? I am often greeted with amazement and surprise, occasionally disbelief, that I made it through the process with my humanity and spirit intact and unscathed.

It's hard for me to come up with a brief, definitive answer. In a way I believe I was born to do exactly what I do and that the choices I've made were ultimately leading me in this direction. As a child I was fascinated with nature and science. I also loved people, especially children. At ten years of age these two factors led me to decide I wanted to become a physician. From that time on, I never wavered in my career choice. I grew up at a time where there were prominent images of the physician. Also, my parents instilled in me a sense of responsibility in terms of making a contribution and giving something back to my community.

After three years, I completed my degree requirements and left Brown during my junior year to attend Duke University's School of Medicine. Duke had an outstanding reputation as a major medical institution. The year I entered it was ranked third in the country.

I clearly recall my first day of medical school. For me, it was filled with excitement and a nervous anticipation. Little did I know what I was getting myself into. Yet I knew even then I was on my way to meet my destiny. We were greeted by the deans and administrators of the school. Of all the speeches and welcomes I heard on that day, the one I most clearly remember was given by Dr. Jay Arena, professor emeritus of pediatrics. He had just returned from a historic trip to China with a group of distinguished Americans. It was a landmark event that was preceded only a few months earlier by President Nixon's trip to China.

In his speech Dr. Arena promised us that our lives would never be the same. At the time I didn't know how right he was. He talked about his trip to China and the humbling experiences he'd had with barefoot doctors who provide so much care to their patients. He remarked that we as future American physicians could learn a lot from their example and should incorporate as much of our humanity as possible into our practice of medicine.

When I entered medical school I was very idealistic and filled with great expectations. I believed in the images and myths of modern medicine. But the realities were vastly different from my expectations. It was a rude awakening to say the least. Becoming a physician was a difficult and arduous process. The sacrifices medical students, interns, residents, and practicing physicians make are unbelievable. On a daily basis they are stretched beyond the limitations of endurance, both physically and psychologically.

When a man or woman enters medical school, the next seven to ten years of his or her life is dominated by medicine. The daily demands are so great they are difficult to perceive for someone who didn't participate in the process. The fear of failure, the physical, emotional, and mental demands are at times unbearable. Exposure to toxic substances, radiation, and contagious disease are all areas of concern.

Medical school was filled with unending stress, contradictions, and disillusionment. Students suffer from information overload. The academic demands are unbelievable. From the first lecture to the last day we were constantly overwhelmed by the load. Classes and labs were held every day from nine to five. To keep up with our daily assignments, the evenings and weekends were filled with intense concentration and study.

During my first term I recall a physiology lecture on the functioning of the heart. I remember marveling at the professor's remarks and wondering in the midst of his discussion how the spirit interacts with the body. I wanted to know what role it played. But at the time, in my heart I knew it would be a long while before I had an opportunity to find the answer to that question.

It was a challenge and test of the will to keep up with the volume of information we were required to assimilate on a daily basis. In the beginning it was an exhilarating experience for me. I was fascinated with the way the body functioned. Studying the various disciplines—including anatomy, physiology, microbiology, pathology, biochemistry, histology, and genetics—intrigued me.

Our education centered around the continuous regurgitation of incoherent facts and frequently unrelated theories. Competition was extreme. Medical students quickly learned that looking good for the professors and attending physicians was the order of the day.

In the world of medicine, everything pales before data. The communicative doctor-patient relationship that is the foundation of a medical practice has been overshadowed by the physician's focus on scientific data. Quite simply, doctors are taught to be scientists. The medical environment is not conducive to the humanistic aspects of patient care. Time and time again doctors are forbidden by example and reprimands from becoming emotionally involved with their patients on any level.

Because of my perspective it was difficult for me to function in such a restrictive environment. I had to learn how to accommodate my personality without losing a sense of who I was. I absolutely refused to become lost in being *Dr. Ferguson*. One of those challenging moments happened when I had my first face to face contact with a dying patient.

Barbara was a young woman in her late twenties suffering from malignant melanoma, the most fatal form of skin cancer. As part of the requirement for my psychiatry clinical rotation during my second year at Duke, I had to interview a patient on the wards to determine whether there were any clinical signs of psychiatric disease.

She sat listlessly on her bed, as she spoke of finding the first tumor on her leg. Surgery had failed to stop the progression of the disease and she was rapidly approaching the terminal phase. She calmly talked about her disease and impending death, almost without any emotion. She said that she was not afraid of dying and was primarily concerned about her two small children. She knew her husband was not prepared to take care of them. She was convincing up to a point, but I didn't feel she was totally prepared to die, nor was I prepared to deal with a dying patient. I was shaken by our conversation. It was the first time in my life I had a conversation of that type with a dying person. I'd seen relatives dying, like my grandmother, but they were older people and had lived full lives. Here was a young woman, maybe eight or nine years my senior, who was preparing to meet death.

Because I had yet to really consider my own mortality in depth, after our interview I left the hospital and rushed to the gardens located behind it. I sat there amidst the flowers for at least a half hour thinking about Barbara, feeling extremely sorry and sad for her, and to an extent feeling her pain as if it were my own. As I sat there, I felt so impotent. There was nothing I or anyone else could do for her.

The Inhumanity of Being "Objective"

Later that day, I ran into one of my residents and asked him how he dealt with dying patients. "I don't think about it. And after a while you won't either," he replied. "It's a fact of life, simple as that." I was saddened by his reaction. But to be honest, I really didn't expect much more. Since starting my clinical rotations I was beginning to see how the process affected doctors—its potential for creating emotional distance between the doctor and patient, and the toll it took on the physician. I saw this evolution in the faces of so many of my classmates. At times it was very frightening. But it did not happen to everyone.

We were taught one of the most important aspects of being a physician was to maintain at all times, and seemingly at all costs, a distant, *objective*, and uninvolved approach to our patients. We were taught to palpate, not to touch. To hear, not to listen. To analyze, not to understand. To be scientific, not to be humane; to be intellectual, rather than emotional; and to be detached, instead of getting involved. The educational process often leads to a sarcastic, cynical perspective, plus emotional and physical instabilities.

We quickly learned that emotional involvement was wrong, that caring was frivolous, and compassion was unnecessary. To allow anything to interfere with the scientific approach was likened to a traitorous act. Conversations were only for the sake of gaining information concerning a patient's condition, not for expressing any genuine concern and care for a fellow human being.

I found the irony of this grossly inhumane process overwhelming. In the midst of a dehumanizing atmosphere and environment, we were learning how to treat our fellow human beings. Because modern medicine has a very objective, technology-oriented and impersonal approach, the contradictions merge in a variety of ways, including the way doctors are trained to perform and the way patients are treated more like walking specimens than human beings.

Yet there were some shining examples of physicians who'd managed to remain compassionate, caring, and very humane healers. Ironically the students and residents tended to gravitate towards them. I once heard a world renowned cancer surgeon talk about an experience he had in medical school that dramatically transformed his professional behavior. This doctor talked about how he tried to impress his resident and attending physician by adapting their arrogant and condescending attitude toward an elderly female patient. He said he'd never forget the way he felt afterwards. He was embarrassed and ashamed of the way he'd treated someone who was old enough to be his grandmother. He knew better and became committed to giving his patients the consideration and respect they deserved.

One of the major tenets of modern medicine is *Primum non nocere* — Latin for, *First, do no harm*. I contend we do harm when we withdraw our compassion and concern for the welfare of another human being. I believe when we're distant we assist the process of creating isolation and despair within our patient. When we treat our patients in an *objective* manner, ignoring our common humanity, we deny ourselves and the other person the warmth of sharing in the midst of disease, pain, confusion, and despair.

The attitudes and expectation of physicians have a profound influence on their patients' outcome. Studies show a sense of hopelessness can be transferred to the patient — so can an optimistic attitude. One of our most renowned professors at Duke, Dr. Stead, taught students it was vital to know as much as possible about the patient's life in order to gain insight and an understanding of the impact the disease had upon his or her life, family, and community.

I love people and interacting with them, so I was fascinated by the progress of many patients. It was awesome to watch a patient who was expected to die, recover and go home. Even more remarkable were the rare occurrences of spontaneous remissions of terminal diseases. These patients confused and stupefied my teachers, because they could not explain what happened in terms of their reductionistic approach. For me, they were a source of inspiration that sparked my inquisitive nature. I wanted to know more.

One study conducted at Massachusetts General Hospital found that a brief visit with an anesthesiologist that gave patients information concerning the potential complications and side effects of anesthesia and surgery significantly reduced the complications and hospitalization period. This was in contrast to patients who had the same surgery, but were not visited.

After completing medical school, I decided to return to the Midwest. I began my residency training at the University of Chicago's Wyler Children's Hospital. Those three years were the most grueling and difficult I've ever experienced. Working on the average of 100 to 120 hours a week was at times, unbearable. But because I enjoyed taking care of children, I found ways to cope with the demands of my job.

Intuition as a New Dynamic

During my training I began to have very lucid, intuitive experiences about my patients. I didn't understand what was going on, however, and it puzzled me. For example, one day while on the wards I began to have a pervading feeling of death. I couldn't pinpoint it, but I knew someone was about to die. A few minutes later, I overheard another intern talking about one of his cancer patients. Amy was almost six years old, had leukemia, and was in remission. She was in for chemotherapy, and her heart was beginning to weaken from the toxicity of the drugs. In less than three hours she went into complete heart failure and died.

It happened again a couple of years later. I was a senior resident on call one night in the intensive care nursery. My intern and I finally got to catch a little sleep. At about 1:30 A.M. I sat up in my bed and felt the need to go check on one baby. So I reluctantly woke Brett and asked him to accompany me back into the nursery.

"Why do you want to check on that baby, Elaine? He's stable and this is the first night in days we've actually gotten some sleep," he replied grumpily.

"Brett just humor me, OK?"

As we were walking out of the on call room, the nurse taking care of this baby was on her way to get us. He had suddenly taken a turn for the worse and his life support systems needed to be adjusted.

The next day Brett commented to me, "Elaine, that was really weird. How did you know something was wrong with that baby?"

"I don't know, I just felt as if something was wrong."

A few months later, when Brett and I were back on the wards, we had an unusual case. A young boy was admitted to our cardiology service on a night we were off duty. He had a collection of fluid surrounding his heart. The attending physicians were called in that night for an emergency consultation and a diagnosis of systemic juvenile rheumatoid arthritis was made. None of his test results were significant, except for a minor abnormality noted in his spine.

After several days Peter's condition slowly declined. He was not responding to his medication. No one could figure out why. On morning rounds I was suddenly compelled to ask Brett to do a stronger test for tuberculosis on this child.

"Elaine, why do you want to do that? The first one was negative."

"I know. But sometimes the patients can be unresponsive to the skin test. Just do it to humor me."

The other doctors on the service thought I was off target. One attending physician in infectious disease insisted this child could not have T.B. because he didn't have any risk factors. The cardiologist and rheumatologist were convinced he was just a difficult case of rheumatoid arthritis.

Two days later the skin test was positive. Everyone was shocked and dumbfounded. Except me. I just knew he had it. But what was particularly rewarding about this case was that at least five other people in his family tested positive for it and were treated.

After I completed my residency, I began practicing in Chicago. It was a pleasant change for me, but I was not very satisfied. Over the years I felt as if my talents were not being put to their full use. So I began to investigate other areas of health. I became very interested in nutrition. At the same time, I began to investigate a variety of spiritual traditions and healing techniques that lead me to a holistic way of living and a broader approach to practicing medicine.

Over the years I have investigated and studied a variety of healing techniques. These include laying on of hands, homeopathy, meditations, visualizations, and Reiki. It has been a fascinating and exciting process. My teachers have come from all over the world and have taught me about the different aspects of healing. Each technique I learned contributed to my evolving concept of healing and life. This process has been a wonderful journey, one that has touched and enlightened every part of my life.

Man cures, God heals.
—African proverb

Chapter 4

Healing Defined in Today's Language

Carolyn's voice possessed a noticeably agitated edge. "Dr. Ferguson, I understand you are a holistic doctor. I need your help if you can. I need to have an emotional healing to help me end a very addictive relationship with my boyfriend. Can you help me?" After explaining to her the various types of therapies I use in my practice, we set up an appointment for a couple of days later.

She was still in a very anxious state when she arrived at my office. While taking her history she explained she had been unable to end a long-term relationship, in spite of a sincere desire and recognition of its addictive and unhealthy aspects. After examining Carolyn, we mutually agreed to do a guided meditation with laying on of hands.

The session lasted for about half an hour. Afterwards she noted a wonderful sense of completion, resolution, and peace of mind. She felt a great and painful burden had been lifted. About a week later I received a letter from her repeatedly thanking me for seeing her. She wrote her life had changed dramatically following our session. She found the courage and strength to end the relationship that had plagued her for over five years. She'd become more loving, caring, and nurturing of her own needs.

One year later Carolyn reported the consultation was a turning point in her life. She was certainly one of the most dramatic examples of emotional or physical healing I've had the privilege to witness. Usually the path to healing is a process rather than one spontaneous event.

Since my childhood I have been fascinated by the Biblical accounts of the healings Jesus, the Christ, performed. I wondered about the capacity to heal by a simple touch. I was stimulated even more so during my training when I witnessed many unexplainable instances of spontaneous healing. I wanted to know more about this mysterious and unpredictable occurrence of healing. It confused, confounded, perplexed, and seemingly frightened many of my professors because it didn't fit into their scientific mind-set. I came to see how the mysteries of life, manifesting within the boundaries of birth and death, can stimulate us to seek new vistas of meaning and understanding—or frighten us into refusing to acknowledge their intangible presence.

Challenging Our Belief Systems

Healing, perhaps more so than any other mystery, profoundly challenges the beliefs which have charted our path through life. Healing pierces our carefully assembled veils of belief and layers of perceptions to the core of our being. This miracle often provokes an evaluation of previously automatically accepted beliefs, allowing the opportunity of transcending to a new level of awareness and a deeper understanding of life's true essential nature.

How does a body racked with cancer suddenly lack any trace of disease? Why does a stable patient with a mild, non-threatening infection suddenly die? Why do people frequently have premonitions of their own death?

These are a few of the questions that catapulted me into a fascinating journey to seek a deeper understanding of the true nature of healing. *Healing* was a term rarely used in clinical narratives and discourses. It was reserved for the description of bone and wound regeneration. Other phrases, like *resolution of symptoms, quiescent phase,* and *marked improvement,* were used in its place. Healing is derived from the Anglo-Saxon word *haelen,* which means to make whole. Perhaps my mentors were subconsciously aware that modern medicine's focus on suppressing symptoms rarely promotes healing.

Healing is ultimately an expression and manifestation of love. Love is ultimately the source of all things and all healing. Love is the essence of our spirit. It is the light that embellishes our being with life. Love is the most important force in the universe. It can lift one from disease, isolation,and rejection to healing awareness and joy. Love is liberating and transforming, unhooking the chains that have held us captive to a life of inconsistencies, fragmentation, despair, pain, and disease. There are no limitations to love. Its power should not be overlooked or underestimated.

Today the medical community is beginning to acknowledge the role love plays in our life. Babies die without it, children's growth and development need it, and adults still require it to enhance the purpose and meaning of life.

We all need love, regardless of who we are, irrespective of position or status. It's what makes our world go round. Mahatma Gandhi once said, "Love is the most powerful force in the world, yet it is the humblest imaginable." Love is a palpable force—an energy that profoundly facilitates the healing process.

Healing supports the return of our conscious a-wareness of the harmonious state of being and the radiant light of our spirit within. This is the place where disease, disharmony, distress, and pain are not known. And the path of healing is an inseparable part of life that is unique for each of us. It entails different aspects and levels of our being.

For some it happens spontaneously, while for most of us it takes months, years, even decades. The length of time healing requires is not important: the fact it occurs is what is essential. It empowers and facilitates the progress towards wholeness. We all have the capacity to heal—to transform and transcend the physical, emotional, and mental parameters that has seemingly locked us into fragmentation, despair, rejection, and fear.

With each encounter I came to see there was an intangible, undefinable aspect to healing—the radiance of an inner peace, ushered forth perhaps by the spirit, beyond the manifestation of body and emotions.

The Gift of Disease

During my years in medical school I was truly amazed by my body's resiliency. Considering all of the insults the body endures during a lifetime, it's surprising to me that disease is not more prevalent or deva-stating. Disease is discerned as any imbalance imped-ing expression of one's physical, emotional, intellectu-al, creative, and spiritual capacities. People afflicted with illness are not considered to be victims of circum-stances. Illness and death are not viewed as punish-ment, but as a portion of life, an event with a myriad of contributing factors and causes, known and un-known.

Frequently there are regressions of illness and the disappearances of tangible disease. Rarely have I seen a person rejoice when a diagnosis of a serious life-threatening disease was made. One of my patients, Faith, was an exception. For years she had very subtle, confusing, and constantly changing symptoms involving her nervous system. She'd seen close to a dozen doctors in the three years since her symptoms first developed. She was repeatedly told nothing was wrong with her and that it was all in her head.

When she came to see me, she was desperate to know what was happening to her body. After an extensive work-up that took a couple of weeks, a scan of her brain finally answered the question she had longed to know. Faith had multiple sclerosis.

In all honesty, when I received the report, I was hesitant to tell her. I thought the news might have a devastating effect on her. To my surprise, her response was the exact opposite of what I had expected. When I told her she had M.S. she broke down and cried tears of gratitude.

"Thank you, Dr. Ferguson. You've helped me so much. Because now I know what's wrong with me. Now I can begin to heal myself." Over the weeks and months that followed she launched one of the most valiant efforts I've ever seen. She fought back bravely to regain control over her body. And she did. Her disease has been in remission for almost a year.

Blessings in Disguise

Frequently I've had patients tell me after a serious, life-threatening illness is healed that the disease was a blessing in disguise. Healing can manifest at any moment in many ways. Most frequently it begins with a conscious search during a time of emotional, physical, or spiritual upheaval. Disease is part of our internal alarm system. It prompts us to focus our attention on what is out of order within our being. Usually it is preceded by subtle warning symptoms and signs that are often ignored. Illness and disease demand our attention; they cannot be ignored.

The Chinese word for crisis and opportunity are one and the same. The way we react physiologically depends on our perceptions. Illness can be viewed as a friend, a teacher, or a blessing—not necessarily something synonymous with punishment. If we accept it, rather than deny its presence or war with it, healing is usually facilitated.

Crisis is an opportunity for growth, a time that allows the transformation of stumbling blocks into steppingstones. Diseases, imbalances, and challenges exist as a means of stimulating, promoting, prompting, and evoking deeper awareness of self. The ties that inhibit and bind us can become vistas for the expression of our highest good. Yet, because we don't want to suffer, we avoid it. So like a magnet, we attract more and more—aggravating the conditions that lead to healing.

The crisis of disease and the fear of dying—as crippling as they may be—can open the door to a greater understanding of the self, piercing through various aspects of being that have previously been ignored. Disease frequently prompts an evaluation of the past in a different light. This can lead to healing, resolution, and the inner peace that often results in the dissolution of emotional and physical disease.

Since life is a process of continuous change, hallmarked by infinite possibilities for growth and expansion, illness can be an opportunity for the expression of growth as a part of the process of healing. The beliefs and perceptions of the patient and physician determine whether illness is treated indifferently as a punishment or recognized as an opportunity for growth. In the latter the individual's consciousness focuses on the imbalance, which is the womb from which greater awareness and understanding can usher forth.

Often I've talked to terminally ill patients who looked upon their impending death as a form of punishment, failure, or a consequence of wrongdoing. Death is not synonymous with failure. It is an inevitable aspect of life, intricately linked to the way we live and experience our lives. Like disease, it doesn't need to be feared or avoided. It is a powerful reminder of the importance of living each day as fully and as abundantly as possible. And if do, death is simply a birth into another realm. As the soul moves on into the light of another place, it relieves us from the limitations of life and earth.

I once viewed death as a negative experience. That's what I learned in medical school. I've grown to see it is a natural and inevitable part of life. Certainly our days can be shortened by our lifestyle and emotions; they can also be extended. I can't tell you the number of patients I've seen who wanted to die, but were free of disease and illness. Life had become a meaningless, empty void filled with nothing but waiting for a release. These people felt trapped in their own bodies—a fate that was for them, worse than death.

I've been blessed to witness the process of death on several occasions. I've watched people who were in the throes of unrelenting pain and impending death, touch upon and express the underlying wholeness and contentment that had eluded them all their lives. I've seen many die in peace, especially children. It appeared to me their little lives were sheltered from the agony of resentment and regret that frequently makes death so difficult to face.

The inability to resolve physical disease does not always mean healing did not occur. Death and healing are not mutually exclusive. I've seen several patients, during the terminal phase of an illness, experience profound healings that facilitated dying in a state of peace and acceptance. Because healing stems from the spirit, rejuvenating the heart and emotions, it leads to a wholeness and inner peace beyond the physical state of being.

On several occasions I've seen patients dying with hearts radiating immense love and compassion, expressions of the divine inner qualities which frequently remain untapped in life. This was particularly true of children dying from terminal diseases. There was an awesome grace about their presence that was truly something to behold.

During my clinical years in medical school, death was treated as merely the cessation of organ function. My mentors rarely, if ever, considered the role the spirit plays in disease and death. I often wondered what death really was, how it occurred, and what actually happened to the spirit when the body died.

The question, *when does life end?* has been one of the greatest ethical and moral issues of this century. This is particularly true since new technological advancements can now maintain body function for an indefinite period of time. The process of attempting to answer this question and provide guidelines for clinical situations that occur on a daily basis has involved doctors, lawyers, clergy, the judicial branch of our government, and the media.

Because of our focus on the body, the spiritual aspects of being are disregarded while we attempt to discern where to draw the line between life and death. My clinical experience with dying patients led me to see there is no clear division between *life* and *death*. A huge gray area exists; it is a no man's land. Because of the artificial maintenance of bodily function, we frequently don't know if the patient is dead or alive—or what would happen if life support were removed. Usually the patient dies. But sometimes, as was the case with Karen Ann Quinlan, the body regenerates to the point of being able to maintain its function while remaining comatose for years. Rarely there are patients who seemingly return from the grave with all of their faculties intact. Frequently they are renewed by the *near death* experience with a deeper appreciation and understanding of life.

During my last month of residency training, Peter —a 13-year-old adolescent—was admitted to our service in preparation for a kidney transplant. Since his birth, he'd been afflicted with kidney disease. His body had recently rejected the first transplant. The surgery and postoperative period were both smooth and uncomplicated. His new kidney functioned well and there were no signs of impending kidney dysfunction or rejection. About a week after the transplant we began to plan his discharge from the hospital. Then early one morning when I was on call, I was abruptly awakened at 6:15 by a page concerning a cardiac arrest of a child on the third floor. As I rushed from the resident's quarters to the room, little did I know that the child I was scurrying to attend was Peter.

Upon entering the room I saw him lying motionless on his bed. His eyes were fixed into a blank and glazed stare. Nurses, technicians, and my intern were frantically connecting monitors, pumping his chest, and manually ventilating him with a bag. His heart was not beating. His lungs did not respirate without assistance. His body was completely unresponsive to any painful stimulation.

We resuscitated him for at least a half hour, during which time he was given medication to stimulate his heart, as well as electrocardioversion (electrical impulses to shock the heart to beat). Finally, I briefly left the room to notify the attending physician, which is routine procedure with arrests. Dr. Jamison had been Peter's private doctor for many years and had developed a genuine love for him. He was quite upset with the news.

After promising to keep Dr. Jamison posted of any changes in Peter's condition, I rushed back to his room. Nothing had changed. He was still unresponsive, not breathing or having any independent cardiac activity. In spite of his state, we continued vigorous resuscitation for at least 45 more minutes.

It slowly became evident to me and the others in the room that Peter had probably died before we even initiated resuscitation. I left the room once more to notify my attending physician of the situation and to request permission to end the unsuccessful resuscitation effort. Andy, as the residents affectionately called him, was very disheartened. He reluctantly agreed to discontinue treatment. After hanging up the phone and slowly walking back to his room, I heard a nurse scream, "I've got a pulse!" I couldn't believe my ears. Then I cringed, realizing if he was in fact *alive*, severe brain damage had probably occurred.

Within the next few moments we transferred him to the intensive care facility. To our surprise, Peter's heart rate immediately became strong and stable, just as suddenly and mysteriously as it had returned. He was placed on complete life support. About a half hour later, Andy walked into the unit looking for our team to begin morning rounds. He was shocked to discover us hovering over Peter's body. "I thought you said Peter was dead," he said to me. I could only reply, "I thought so, too!"

Several blood samples were drawn to ascertain if there was the presence of a metabolic cause for his arrest and to determine the status of his transplanted kidney. We were looking for any signs of rejection that might have precipitated his arrest. His surgeons believed no demonstrable signs of kidney rejection existed. Over the next few days, all of the test results, with the exception of the electroencephalogram (brain wave test), repeatedly returned within the normal range. Yet Peter remained in a deep, unresponsive coma. The life support system attached to his body was the only thing keeping him alive.

The EEG (brain wave test) revealed minimal brain function and the likelihood of severe brain damage was evident. We were all convinced if he did survive, he would have a serious neurological impairment due to the brain's prolonged period of oxygen deprivation. In rounds we imagined if he came out of the coma he would have to learn to live with blindness, deafness, or limited use of his limbs.

For several days Peter remained in a deep coma. On the seventh day after the arrest, on an otherwise uneventful afternoon, he suddenly sat up in his bed. Still connected to total life support, he yanked the endotracheal tube from his throat in order to speak. He told us about a beautiful place he'd visited, and of wonderful feelings of joy and love he had experienced in this place. He recalled consciously deciding to return to this life because he was a bit homesick and missed his friends.

Transformation and the Process of Healing

Healing, health, and transformation are all aspects of the same process—expressions of the spirit. Like light refracted into a rainbow, the spirit of healing reflects in many ways from the part of our being that is inextricably linked to all of life. Healing rests in the spirit, a place of peace beyond the dualities of our world.

Healing is a transformative, life changing process. It takes us to our core—an intrinsic wholeness where we are not diseased, wounded, or alone. It takes us to the place within all of us where there is nothing but love.

Transformation is not merely change. It harmonizes and heals the irregularities of our being that are out of alignment with our highest good. True healing, a process of change, facilitates the expressions of our wholeness. It facilitates self-awareness. It allows us to express our greatest capacity on each and every level. This process leads us to heightened awareness, where spirit meets life, body, emotions, and thoughts. Through love it brings them into accord with our spirit. Thus the disparities, the pain, the discomfort, and the disease are transformed. If we seek only to quiet and suppress our pain, rather than to heal and resolve it, then we will be distracted from our higher purposes in life.

Transformation involves all levels of being. It is not limited to the body. It moves beyond that realm—allowing the expression of our spirit to permeate into our bodies, minds, and hearts. This leads to a greater awareness of life and promotes well-being. It opens the heart and mind to the moment, allowing us to live in harmony and a growing appreciation and awareness of life.

Because of its transformative aspects, life after healing is never the same. One truly can't return to the ways of the past. Like a snake shedding old skin that is no longer of use, or the butterfly emerging from its cocoon, there is a newness of life that occurs with healing. Nothing is the same. Everything changes as one's being and perceptions are infused by love. The search for this sense of self, for inner harmony of the fragmented parts of being, is the foundation and focus of our spiritual quest. It ultimately results in the discovery that great wisdom lies within.

I once had a patient, a young woman in her late twenties, who had a mild case of pericarditis, which is an inflammation of the heart muscle. Usually once every two or three years she had debilitating episodes of severe chest pain that required hospitalization. This had to be followed by several weeks of bed rest. The cause of Jackie's disease was never identified. For several years she was in remission and led a normal life. Then it suddenly and dramatically flared up again. When she was hospitalized her situation was complicated by the discovery of another heart condition that involved a malfunctioning valve.

Jackie did well during her hospitalization and was discharged on medications treating both conditions. Within two weeks she returned to her daily routine. She stopped coming to the office for her scheduled visits. After awhile, I called her to find out how she was doing.

"Dr. Ferguson, I'm fine. I haven't come to see you because I now understand what causes my heart to get sick," she replied. "You see, when I was in the hospital I thought about the times I've had flare-ups. They happen after I've had a serious emotional upheaval. The last time it happened I had a big fight with my boyfriend. It actually wasn't a fight, it was just the worse verbal abuse I've ever endured in my life. And it happened because someone gave him a hard time on his job.

"So he decided once again he had the right to abuse me. I'm not taking that anymore. Even though I love him, my health is far more important than he could ever be," she continued. "I knew I had to let go of him in order to maintain my health. When I left, the symptoms improved quickly, much faster than ever before. The pain went away. I'm fine."

Throughout my many years of training and practicing I have witnessed many other incidents of miraculous healing and seen diseases spontaneously disappear. I have also watched stable patients promptly take a dramatic turn for the worse and suddenly die without any warning. These experiences lead me to seek an understanding of healing and to find methods to assist the body's vast capacity to heal itself.

Man is made by his belief, as he believes—so he is.
—Bhagavad Gita

Chapter 5

The Unity of Body, Mind and Spirit

Shortly after I began practicing medicine I ran into the teenage granddaughter of one of my patient's while shopping one evening at a major department store in downtown Chicago. Mrs. Giles was probably the most complicated patient I had at the time. She had insulin dependent diabetes, severe heart disease, limited kidney function, arthritis, and hypertension. She was usually hospitalized once a year with severe chest pain to rule out a heart attack. And during the interim she remained relatively stable.

She'd missed her last appointment and I wanted to know how she was doing. "Tracy, I haven't seen your grandmother in a while, how is she?" "Dr. Ferguson, she's fine. Grandmother only gets sick when she's emotionally upset."

"What do you mean Tracy?" I asked. "Well, whenever we have family problems, especially when someone doesn't do what she expects them to do, she gets upset and very frustrated. Within a couple of days she's having chest pain and usually goes in the hospital.

"It's something everyone in the family has started to notice, because I pointed it out. So we all try hard not to upset her as much as we once did. That way she won't have to go to the hospital."

At the time I made a mental note of Tracy's observations. While I found it interesting, I was too steeped in the traditional view of modern medicine to see how astute this teenager's observations were. What Tracy and her family recognized has been known throughout the world for ages. It is being recognized and acknowledged in a new light in the West. This new field of research, which has emerged during the latter part of the twentieth century, allows us to see the roles emotions, personalities, and reaction to stress play in the maintenance of health and development of disease.

Holistic and Rational
Perspectives of the Mind

Eastern spiritual traditions have always considered the mind to be a doorway leading to greater spiritual, mental, and emotional awareness and physical well-being. For thousands of years healers have used meditation and imagery to augment other techniques to promote healing. The ancient Greek physicians used healing and meditative practices that were passed on to them by the Egyptians.

The writings of Hippocrates contained observations noting certain personality traits that were more common in persons inflicted with cancer. This remains válid today. Because he was heavily influenced by Egyptian medicine, he considered health to be a state of internal and external harmony, with the self and environment. In his approach to treating any illness and disease—the mind, body, and spirit were all viewed as one unit.

Until the mid-seventeenth century, when Descartes' theory emerged concerning the innate distinction and separation of the mind and body, the views of other more organic and holistic approaches were disregarded. As mentioned earlier, the influence of Rene Descartes' belief that the mind and body were separate entities considerably influenced Western scientific thinking. The distinction between mind and body, spirit and matter was complete. The body and mind were completely alienated in Western scientific thought. It is ironic that without proof the theories of Descartes and others were so quickly accepted and integrated into Western thought.

Since then, the role the mind played has been largely ignored and obscured by the focus on identifying external, disease-causing agents. Throughout this century medical literature has been filled with reports, case studies, and research findings that clearly and definitively illustrate the influence the mind, emotions, and beliefs have upon diseases. As early as the beginning of this century, physicians were noticing the role emotional states played in the development of disease.

In 1909, Sir William Osler, one of the founding fathers of modern medicine noted, "The care of tuberculosis depends more on what the patient has in his head than what he has in his chest." Until recently the significance of these reports have been mostly disregarded or ignored by the medical mainstream. These findings have been frequently rejected, while unproven theories have been treated as facts. Proponents have resisted accepting the scientific proof that is accumulating concerning the link of mind and body. The doctors and scientists that have dared to suggest the integrity of body and mind have been subjected to vehement opposition, ridicule, and even ostracism.

The reductionist view was continued by Koch, an eighteenth century scientist, who postulated that a disease was caused by a specific disease-causing agent. The focus was to identify the cause of disease. This belief led to the birth of a particular form of scientific investigation that continues today. Western science has tended to view phenomena in terms of absolutes, seeking to identify one cause. While physicians and other health professionals with a more holistically oriented view recognize there are many significant factors, rather than just one ultimate cause.

Especially during the 1980's, there was a virtual explosion of scientific findings and studies which showed a much closer body-mind relationship than previously believed. The evidence continues to mount supporting the role and influence our emotions have upon our bodies. The mind-body interface is currently one of the most fertile hot beds of scientific investigation. The conclusive findings continue to prompt the reconsideration of many of science's time honored theories that have guided Western thought and its approach to the body for almost four centuries. Because of the growing volume of information demonstrating the integrity of body, mind, and spirit, many mainstream scientists are beginning to lower their resistance to these findings. A new field of scientific investigation has emerged.

Researchers continue to probe the mysteries of the mind. They seek to discover the way emotions, thoughts, and perceptions affect and trigger the physiological and biochemical changes that prevent or render the body more susceptible to disease. Because of these efforts there's been a gradual shift in the way Western physicians and scientists perceive the mind and body. They are beginning to acknowledge the integrity and unity of the two and the powerful force of the mind that previously was cloaked with mystery in the West.

In all honesty, the mind can't be viewed in an isolated fashion as a separate entity, but a part of our being, one that is in continuity with the body and the spirit.

The Body As a Whole

Earlier in the twentieth century scientists began to disregard the mechanical, rational approach. Holistic ideas began to emerge. Dr. Walter Cannon, a Harvard physiologist, proposed the notion that the body maintained a state of *homeostasis*—a self-maintaining harmonious condition that responded to internal and environmental factors. He believed the personality was the controlling and regulatory aspect of the body. In a similar vein, physiologist and biologist Claude Bernard proposed the function of the body was to maintain balance with itself and that imbalance leads to sickness and death.

Around the same time Dr. Franz Alexander renewed the important notion that many chronic disturbances are not caused by external, mechanical factors, but rather are due to continuous functional stress. This led to the development of the concept of psychosomatic medicine. Initially doctors were not willing to accept this concept. But in light of the obvious and unavoidable role emotions played in the genesis and course of these diseases, the concept of psychosomatic medicine was gradually accepted. Medicine gradually recognized the role psychological components played in the course of seven *psychosomatic diseases*. These included ulcers, hypertension, rheumatoid arthritis, hyperthyroidism, neurodermatitis, asthma, and ulcerative colitis. These seven diseases were deemed the only ones that were impacted by emotions.

After these theoretical developments occurred, other scientists began to take another look at the physiology of humans and animals. One of the researchers conducting the most significant work was Hans Selye, a Swiss scientist at McGill University. He made a significant discovery, identifying the basis of the physiologic response to stress.

Selye studied the response elicited by the brain and clearly demonstrated the biochemical and physiologic patterns of normal stress response in animals. His research showed how the hypothalamus—a part of the brain—acts as a bridge between the mind, emotions, thoughts, endocrine system, and peripheral nervous system. This organ controls many physical sensations—such as thirst, hunger, and the sexual drive. It also regulates the pituitary gland. The hypothalamus mediates these responses through releasing hormones that monitor the autonomic nervous system and endocrine system, preparing the body's response to stressful events by stimulating the *fight or flight* response, a primitive animal reaction.

The fight or flight response is a state of protective arousal. It is an instinctive response to life threatening situations and acts as an internal alarm system. The entire physiology is launched into a heightened state, preparing it to do battle. The hypothalamus in the brain triggers the adrenal's response, causing the release of stress-related hormones. This includes cortisol, which affects the biochemistry and physiology of the entire body.

During the 1940's Walter Hesse, another physiologist, also studied the hypothalamus. He found stimulating different sections of the hypothalamus could produce two diametrically opposed states: one of deep relaxation or an alert, heightened flight or fight response. The relaxed response is a protective, healing mechanism, promoting physiologic restoration.

The Birth of a New Scientific Field

In addition to failing to see the link between body and mind, each organ system was believed to function independent of the others, rather than as an integral unit or a dynamic whole. Until recently, for instance, doctors believed the immune system functioned separately and was not influenced by the mind or other organs in the body.

This view is beginning to change. The role emotions play in health and disease continue to be uncovered by scientists throughout the world. Medical literature contains many cases of patients who demonstrated the influence of emotions on disease.

Many early studies and case reports exhibit the influence of the mind on disease states. Yet its potential for healing was overlooked by mainstream physicians. The effect of the mind on the brain—in particular the hypothalamus—as well as communication from the immune system to the brain, has been documented. The work of many scientists now makes it clear that beliefs have a lot more to do with health and disease than the West formerly believed. The mind exerts a tremendous effect upon the physiologic response to stress!

The Wonderful Immune System

The immune system is responsible for protecting the body from invasion by any foreign object, including bacteria, viruses, parasites, chemicals, and airborne pollen substances. It also recognizes the difference between the body and foreign objects, preventing the body from turning on itself. Unlike other organ systems, it lacks an identifiable center and is composed of various parts of the body. Included are the thymus gland, lymph nodes, the spleen, white blood cells, immunoglobulin, and proteins that help ward off infection. The immune system has a dynamic, self-determining, and self-regulating character.

In 1964 George Solomon, a pioneer researcher in the field of immunology at UCLA and the father of the concept, gave his area of investigation the name *psychoimmunology*. It was later renamed *psychoneuroimmunology*. He and his coworkers were the first Americans to report that stress suppressed the immune function in laboratory animals, while early handling of stress enhanced the immune system. Because of his efforts, and those of other scientists throughout the world, a new field of investigation has emerged.

Pschyoneuroimmunology studies the impact the mind, emotions, thoughts, and personality traits have upon the nervous and the immune systems. Psychoneuroimmunology offers the possibility of explaining the way the brain and mind impact upon our bodies in determining the balance of health and illness. It is a multi-disciplinary approach investigating the role the brain and mind play in the resistance or susceptibility to disease in the constantly changing balance of health and illness.

This area of investigation encompasses a variety of topics—imagery, meditation, psychosocial factors, emotional factors, psychotherapy, biofeedback, hypnosis, and relaxation. Psychologists, psychiatrists, social psychologists, immunologists, behaviorists, and neuroendocrinologists conduct the investigation. According to Solomon, the preponderance of evidence links both the central and autonomic nervous system with the immune system beyond a reasonable doubt. He believes all disease results from an interaction of many factors including genetic, endocrine, nervous, immune, and psychological.

While many of the investigations were initially ignored or considered in an adversarial fashion, today even the greatest skeptics and most doubtful observers are beginning to reconsider their rigid stance. Mounting evidence shows the powerful influence the mind and psychological characteristics and qualities have in terms of altering a variety of physiologic responses within the body. This is now well documented. Their roles in the creation of health and the genesis of disease continues to be unveiled in an understandable fashion.

For example, during the 1940's one of the initial studies that discerned the link between the hypothalamus and the immune system occurred quite serendipitously. When Russian scientists destroyed the hypothalamus in rats, they found the animals died at a very rapid rate due to the suppression of the immune system. Several bidirectional pathways of communication between the brain and the immune system have been discovered. And certain chemicals produced by the immune system impact upon the brain and nervous system. Scores of studies have now found an apparent correlation between emotional states and altered responses of the immune system. This opens exciting possibilities for AIDS sufferers, among others.

The Physiological Impact of Thoughts and Emotions

We now know the disease causing agent is only part of the story. The development of disease is not that simple. Everyone exposed to a cold virus, for instance, doesn't get a cold. No one knows precisely the extent that the mind exerts an effect on the body.

It is variable and must be considered in light of other factors. Imprecise and difficult to measure, more significant in different states of mind, it varies from person to person.

The ancients noted that health and disease are dynamic, complex, fluid, and constantly changing processes. Today contemporary physicians recognize the same. Modern medicine is beginning to acknowledge the significant, but variable impact physical, psychological, environmental, and spiritual factors have upon health and disease.

This represents great strides. When I was in medical school we were taught there were only seven psychosomatic diseases that were affected by emotions. During our clinical rotations on the hospital wards, I recall several occasions when medical students would ask a question or suggest a patient's course was affected by psychoemotional factors. The attending physicians and residents completely ridiculed such notions.

Many now believe emotions are the key to health and the very doorway to disease. They are the lens that colors our perceptions of ourselves and our world. Feelings may organize the mind and personality; finely tuned emotions may be the basis of all we know. All thoughts and memories are coded by subtle feeling tones that accompany perception. Thoughts are not purely intellectual, but are embedded in emotional codes. Feeling tones serve to integrate the formation of thoughts; personality structure to code memory. Even before we register it, our perceptions are colored by emotions. Emotions are indeed the key to health.

Stress has captured considerable attention in our modern society. It has been the source of numerous scientific studies, newspaper reports, television specials, and workshops. The level of stress continues to increase at a seemingly accelerated pace in the workplace, in our homes, and in society in general. Quite simply, we live in a world where the levels of stress appear to accelerate on a daily basis. Stress is a buzz word for most people. Many are stretched to the point of burn-out. To cope with this anxiety, last year over 144 million new drug prescriptions were written. The three best selling drugs were all used in the treatment of stress-related disorders. Millions take tranquilizers and mood-altering drugs to deal with the chronic stresses in their lives, while others participate in stress reduction and relief programs.

In 1956 when Hans Selye wrote a landmark book, *The Stress of Life*, he described the characteristics of stress as an unavoidable aspect of life, a response to the daily changes of life and the body's non-specific reaction to any demand made upon it. We now know the choices we make in terms of our perceptions, attitudes, beliefs, and emotions affect the body's physiologic responses. Our thoughts and emotions affect and stimulate the release of hormones as the hypothalamus governs the way the body responds to stress.

Stress is not the issue, our response to it is. Our reaction to acute stress produces physiological changes from which the body easily recovers. Attitudes of helplessness in the face of chronic stress, however, interfere with our natural restorative capacity. Our emotions, thoughts, and attitudes determine our physiologic response toward a stressful situation. There is a two way system of communication linking our mind—the mechanism through which our emotions, our hopes, and our fears can and do affect the body's ability to defend itself—and our physical being.

Our thoughts and emotions trigger the release of hormones in the hypothalamus that governs the way our entire physiology responds to stress. A negative response taxes the body. A positive response brings about wellness and balance. It is the way we respond that determines stress. Stress without *dis*tress promotes wellness and balance. What is the difference between the two? The only difference is the way in which we respond. It determines the influence stress will have upon our physical, emotional, and mental well-being. What we perceive as stressful stimulates the flight or fight response in humans. Different areas of the hypothalamus are stimulated by emotional and mental responses to stress. The areas of the brain controlling emotions are especially rich in receptors for these chemicals. The brain has receptors for chemical compounds produced by the immune system. The excessive release of stress hormones, secondary to stimulation by the hypothalamus, releases cortisol and catecholamines—which impact upon the immune system by depressing the production of antibodies and interfering with the functions of other components. This renders the body more susceptible to a variety of diseases.

Negative emotions trigger a variety of physiological responses, including the release of norepinephrine, a chemical messenger known to suppress immune function. Even if the original stress is alleviated, the size of an advanced malignancy may overwhelm the immunologic response. On the other hand, a positive response to stressful situations helps to perpetuate balance and wellness. It is the way we respond that determines the development of distress and well-being. The only difference in the two is the way we respond. The chronic stimulation of the flight or fight response taxes the body. According to Candace Pert, the Chief of Brain Biochemistry at the National Institute of Mental Health, "The same chemicals that control mood in the brain control the tissue integrity of the body." She has conducted a considerable amount of investigation and study of mind-body interface and the role the mind has upon it. She is one of the leading researchers in psychoneuroimmunology. Our thoughts have an electrical component that can literally impact upon the direction of our physiology.

Scores of studies have found a correlation between emotional states and altered responses of the immune system. The increased incidence of death among widowers, for instance, is related to a depressed immune function. Resilient personalities can enhance immunity. Stressful times result in depressed immunity.

A Harvard study of medical students watching a touching, emotion-filled video about Mother Teresa found that significant increases occurred in the levels of a particular type of antibody that is the first line of defense against invading organisms. There were significant increases in the levels of the IGA antibody, a class that is particularly protective in the lining of the intestinal and respiratory tracts. IGA plays an important role in warding off invasive bacteria.

In another study of students, researchers found this antibody level dropped precipitously during stressful final exam periods. Levels were taken before, during, and after exams. In comparison to the levels obtained before the beginning of the tests, the examination period levels were significantly lower. A study of 111 college students discovered psychologically healthy students were more capable of warding off infection, in comparison to students who were maladjusted to college life.

These investigations have been a source of controversy. Yet even the greatest skeptics and most doubtful observers are beginning to reconsider their rigid stance under the weight of mounting evidence showing the powerful influence emotions have in the susceptibility, development, and survival rate of a variety of illnesses. The role emotions play in health and disease continues to be unveiled in an understandable and concise fashion. It is now well documented that emotional states can alter a variety of physiologic responses within the body.

Personality, Belief and Disease

There are a score of studies demonstrating the role personality patterns appear to play in the regulation of the immune system and how they can lead to specific disease. Doctors noted a couple of decades ago that higher frequency among patients—those with coronary artery disease and heart attacks—of certain personality traits were more common in comparison to the general patient population. These personality characteristics specifically related to the way the individuals dealt with stress. The type "A" controlling, aggressive, assertive, manipulative character, was at a greater risk than the calmer, more introspective, type "B" personality.

During the mid 1960's Lawrence LeShan found, after conducting interviews with hundreds of cancer patients, there were certain common personality traits. He suggested that people with these traits had a higher incidence of cancer. They were long suffering, emotionally repressed, had low self-esteem, or had experienced a personal loss prior to diagnosis.

Studies have shown the effect personality traits have on long-term cancer survivors. In a study to predict survival time in terms of remission, psychological researchers found classification could predict medical outcomes in 88% of the patients who had a rapidly progressing disease. The most important characteristic coincided with the inability to relieve anxiety or depression. Of those with a fighting spirit, 75% had a positive outcome. Only 46% of the poor copers, those feeling despair and helplessness, survived.

We now know, as did the healers and sages of old, that emotions, beliefs, and attitudes play a significant role in the development of all diseases. Attitude has a potent effect on our capacity to maintain health and develop disease. A defiant fighting spirit can increase longevity. Empowerment and some control, regardless of how small, are important psychological considerations.

During my clinical rotations on the wards at Duke I quickly learned that cancer patients were consistently the nicest patients. Residents and attending physicians frequently commented on the irony that the nicest people contracted the worst and most feared disease. Typically they tried to please everyone else—while overlooking themselves. I recall one patient, a Mr. Rourke, who was admitted to our service with a lot of nonspecific complaints. His local physician recommended that he come to Duke because the doctor couldn't figure out what was wrong with him.

His wife accompanied him to the hospital. Less than six months before his admission Mr. Rourke had retired from his job and was settling into retirement. He was the most pleasant patient on our service, always willing to accommodate us.

After an extensive workup, we discovered he had pancreatic cancer. The type he had was usually fatal, but in light of the size and location of the tumor, we felt that he had at least a year to eighteen months more to live. We told him and his wife. Later that day she caught me in the hallway and asked straight up,

"Is my husband going to die? He's very much afraid of this disease and wants to know the truth." I attempted to carefully reiterate to her that his tumor was inoperable and malignant, but he could live for a long time.

The next afternoon, less than twenty-four hours later, I walked past his room and saw the cleaning staff changing the sheets. I was puzzled and found my intern, asking him where Mr. Rourke was. He said, "Mr. Rourke died this morning." I was dumbfounded.

Everyone else on the service was equally astonished. Later my attending commented how surprised he was. "That man should have lived a lot longer than he did. I don't understand. It seems like he just gave up and died. The cancer was isolated, hadn't spread to any other part of his body. What happened?"

A nurse summed it up quite succinctly. "I think Mr. Rourke died so quickly after he was told he had cancer because he simply gave up hope. He didn't believe he would live very long. And no surprise to me he didn't."

There is consistent evidence that the immune system is suppressed in those who feel unable to cope with adversity. Heavy denial of emotions, repression of expression, and abnormal release of emotions cause physiologic responses that interfere with our natural healing mechanisms. For example, breast cancer patients with a pessimistic outlook concerning recovery had a higher mortality rate. The same has been found to be true of many other diseases.

The findings of one British researcher noted that breast cancer patients frequently have an aversion to the female role, neuroses, and hypochondria. While another study of women suspected of having gynecologic cancer found they had a higher incidence of controlled conforming behaviors, less adventurous natures, are assertive, autonomous, and possess competitive traits. Another prospective study found a specific tendency to bottle up anger correlated with malignancy in 160 women admitted to a London Hospital for biopsy of breast tumors. There was no significant difference in the incidence of depression. Only one-third of those later found to have malignant tumors were judged able to express anger. In general, cancer patients tend to be more depressed than normal people, but not depressed enough to seek therapy.

These personality characteristics and qualities do not suggest that everyone with them will develop cancer or any other disease. They do suggest that there is an increased risk and susceptibility in terms of developing the disease, but this is not an absolute.

They tend to feel helpless, and have a disturbed or emotionally void relationship with parents. They lack satisfactory emotional outlets, bottling or suppressing anger and other strong emotions. They are poor copers and have a great sense of hopelessness and quiet despair—living a life filled with silent anguish and invisible suffering. They typically score above average on a psychological test for depression, but are not severe enough to require professional help.

Cancer frequently occurs after significant life events, like the loss of an important figure: parent, spouse, child, or close friend through death or separation. Such life crises diminish the immune system, and specific mental disorders and severe emotional disturbances are accompanied by abnormalities in the immune system. Early emotional experiences can have a devastating consequence upon the immune system. Monkeys separated from their mothers experience a suppression of their immune system, which improved when placing them again in an active and supportive environment.

Reaction to acute stress produces temporary physiologic changes that the body can easily recover from. It is the chronic attitudes of helplessness in the face of continuous stress that interfere with and deplete our natural restorative capacity. The mind exerts a tremendous effect upon the body's physiologic response to stress. The inability to deal with stress, rather than stress itself, helps trigger the development of cancer in those who've suffered loss. And helplessness may play a key role in susceptibility to cancer, somehow interfering with the ability of the organism to resist tumor development. We know that long-term frustration and chronic hopelessness leads to disease because these emotions impact upon the body in terms of increasing susceptibility through lowering resistance. We also know that receptiveness to change increases resistance to disease and capacity for health, and that the deepest relaxation is being one with yourself and at home in your body. A fighting spirit increases longevity.

Adaptability to Life

Our behaviors, guided by our personality traits, influence the way we live—the way we choose to adapt to life in terms of our flexibility in the face of life's unpredictable trials and tribulations. During the 1970's Caroline Thomas, a researcher at Johns Hopkins University, added weight to this work when she studied and followed a group of more than thirteen hundred Johns Hopkins University medical students between 1948 and 1964. The group reported that had been emotionally distant from one or both parents for more than three decades. In comparison to other groups they had an unusually high incidence of mental illness, suicides and death from cancer. A Harvard

1937 Grant Study, Adaptation to Life, found similar immature coping styles led to disease. Most notably the researchers found individuals who typically handle stress and strain in an immature way also became ill four times more often. They used coping styles characteristically employed by children. These included projection, unconsciously disavowing the conflicting thoughts and feelings, identifying them to be expressed in the behavior or statements of others.

In another study, rats with implanted tumors were shocked. They rejected the tumors more frequently if they were themselves able to end the shocks. In animals and humans, when the source of stress is prolonged or undefined, or when the sources exist concurrently, an individual can't return to a normal state. Similar findings were noted in nursing home patients who felt no control over their daily lives in terms of choices. There was a much higher death rate. Senior citizens allowed to choose their meals and when to make telephone calls decreased their mortality rate by 50% within eighteen months.

As research continues to unlock the mysteries of the mind—and document the integrity of body, mind, and spirit—the opportunities for applying this knowledge and integrating it into the medical mainstream will as well.

> His countenance was like lightning, and his clothes as white as snow.
>
> *—Matthew 28:3*

Chapter 6

The Aura: A Body of Light

Several years ago, before I began to study various spiritual topics, I had a few experiences that were startling and puzzling. These events remained a mystery to me until a few years later during a studying of the *aura*.

While attending a local conference, I saw a man I'd met years earlier. He had a reputation for outstanding professional and civic accomplishments. I noticed hovering over his head a dark, heavy cloud. It was worrisome to me. Within two weeks he was hospitalized. His doctors discovered a rare and very malignant tumor in his abdomen. The cancer had already spread to several sites throughout his body. Less than a year later, Richard succumbed to the disease, quietly dying in his sleep.

A few months later I saw a woman, a very active member of my church who'd recently had open heart surgery due to severe blockage in three arteries. She looked radiant. While talking to her, however, I couldn't help but notice a gray cloud surrounding her body. I felt the presence of death hovering near her. I shrugged my feelings off and thought it was just my imagination. Once again, within a few months Martha developed a malignant tumor in her liver and died less than six months after the diagnosis was made.

The most dramatic experience occurred during the final days of my residency. It happened during morning rounds one Saturday in mid-June with my attending physician and intern present. An eighteen-month old child who was admitted the night before with a mild case of kidney failure was active and playful. The little girl didn't show any physical signs of acute illness. Yet I saw a dense black cloud hovering a few inches above her head. I recall thinking to myself, without any good reason, "You're going to be in the intensive care unit pretty soon."

I didn't really dwell on the occurrence in spite of the fact I'd had several other intuitive incidences during my residency. They all eventually did occur. In light of those experiences, I began to wonder when it would happen.

During the morning, several hours before she was admitted Sonya suddenly developed a very high fever that did not respond to medication. Her mother had noticed during the day that Sonya's diaper remained dry and her appetite was sluggish. Later that evening the little girl was brought to our emergency room and admitted. She had kidney failure and anemia caused by the failure.

This disease was an uncommon form of reversible kidney failure in children. It usually has a brief course, lasting only a few days. Most commonly, children afflicted by it tend to completely recover, without any lasting side effects or significant compromise of their kidney function. The cause is unknown, but experts believe it may be due to an increased sensitivity of the child's immune system that damages the blood and kidneys. Parents frequently recall that their child experienced mild flu symptoms a few weeks before the kidney failure occurred. The sensitivity may have been triggered by the bacteria or virus that caused the flu symptoms.

During her first night in the hospital she had very little urine output, and her kidneys remained in mild failure. Later that day, my chief resident was kind enough to cover for me for a couple of hours in order that I could attend a banquet held in downtown Chicago. Upon my return to the hospital I paged Linnea, our chief resident, to relieve her. She and my intern were in the intensive unit. They were in the process of completing Sonya's transfer to the unit, because of a sudden and critical drop of her blood pressure and heart rate.

Over the course of the next two days Sonya's condition continued to rapidly deteriorate. We were all confused and surprised by her sudden decline. Our kidney specialist was equally baffled. He couldn't understand why her clinical status had worsened so quickly. Aside from dialyzing her blood and providing basic life support, there wasn't much we could do for her.

I continued to see the dark cloud growing and becoming denser. On the following Monday morning I was suddenly paged by the unit. Without warning, Sonya's heart stopped beating. By the time I arrived she was in full cardiac arrest. We vigorously resuscitated her for at least forty-five minutes, to no avail. Throughout the resuscitation she remained completely unresponsive. In spite of all of our efforts to save her, she was pronounced dead shortly before noon, less than two and a half days after she was admitted.

Because I never understood the significance of the dark clouds, they continued to baffle and frustrate me. My focus at that time was completely scientific in light of my training. I really didn't know what I had seen or

anything about an *aura*. I decided to forget about
these experiences. Many years and countless experiences would occur before I discovered the significance
and meaning of these phenomena.

What is the Aura?

Since time immemorial men and women have
individually and collectively considered the physical
body as one component of their existence. Generation
upon generation has believed their existence was
inextricably linked to and dependent upon an underlying spiritual element for life and expression. Life on
earth was viewed as a temporary existence marked by
continuous change. By virtue of the various life experiences encountered, incarnation afforded the soul—the
divine, eternal, and unchangeable essence of being—
with continuous opportunities to grow and expand its
awareness in wisdom, in truth, and in love.

Today most people throughout the world firmly
believe we are more than our bodies. Like our ances-
tors they think we are in the presence of an inextricable spiritual, essential, and unseen dimensions of
being.

Throughout the ages cultures and traditions have
recognized and revered the presence of a sphere of
light surrounding and penetrating the body. The aura,
the Latin word meaning *glowing light*, is recognized as
the form which allows the manifestation and expression of the spirit in the material world. It plays a
significant role in physical, emotional, and spiritual
development—in health, disease, and healing.

Our culture is filled with references to the aura,
particularly in terms of religious paintings depicting
light surrounding the heads of spiritual leaders. Children frequently describe colors surrounding bodies

and other objects that are consistent with various aspects of the aura. Because parents and other adults are usually not aware of the aura, they disregard the children's descriptions, attributing their comments to a vivid imagination.

Today scientists throughout the globe are researching and studying various aspects of the aura and other related phenomena, including a universal field of energy that links all of creation together. The aura is the portion of this field primarily responsible for the expression of human life. Scientists have confirmed its presence, as well as certain nonvisible structures within the aura that are consistent with ancient descriptions of the aura.

These and other findings are the foundations of a new field of medicine. It is emerging due to accumulating information which opens the possibilities of incorporating all the spiritual aspects into modern medicine.

Historical Perspectives of the Aura

From the ancient Egyptians to our present age, the vast majority of the world's spiritual and religious traditions have recognized the presence of a sphere of light penetrating and surrounding the body. This radiant body of light is the vehicle that facilitates the soul's manifestation in the material world, investing the physical form with life, vitality, and creative expression. The aura is the vehicle through which the soul expresses and manifests life in the physical world. It monitors the orderly transmission of universal energies from higher planes, systematically stepping down the vibrations for entry into the physical body. This human energy system continuously provides the vital energies necessary for nourishment of the body's cells, tissues, and organs. It forms an egg shaped sphere around the body.

From the moment of conception, the aura acts as a blueprint for the physical form, guiding and directing the development, organization, and function of the internal organs. In health, a harmonious balance exists between the energies of the aura, the physical body, and the forces of the environment.

Before the expression of disease occurs in the physical body, there is a disruption and blockage of flow within the aura. Emotional, mental, physical, or spiritual imbalance or distress are the most common causes of blocks. Depending on the severity and the duration of the blockage—as well as the individual's ability to restore the normal flow and balance in the aura—there is an increased likelihood that the person will develop physical and/or emotional disease.

Clairvoyants, mystics, and healers throughout the ages have consistently described it. Through assessing various aspects and qualities of it, they have discerned an individual's state of health, emotions, and predisposition to disease. They note dynamic changes in the aura coinciding with emotional and physical states, relationships, and environment. During the twentieth century several researchers have substantiated the aura's presence. That a psychic can accurately describe the vibrational frequencies and the expansive interplay of these energies is a fact and not subjective judgment. They have also confirmed that a relationship actually exists between emotional states and the colors of the aura.

It is through the aura that healers and other *vibrational* therapies stimulate and augment the body's natural healing process, correcting abnormal vibrational patterns that block the flow of energies of higher frequencies that are necessary for the normal functioning. Laying on of hands, acupuncture, homeopathy, flower essences, and other vibrational therapies all stimulate the natural healing process by correcting blocks and other irregularities in the function and regulation of the cells and organs and behaviors.

Scientists have recently discovered all living organisms emit low intensity light which can be measured by counting light particles or measuring electromagnetic waves. The physical body is the densest and least permanent of the bodies of man. Because the aura vibrates at higher frequencies than the physical form, its radiant emissions overshadow the light beaming from physical form—similar to how the moon periodically eclipses the light of the sun.

Although the terminology used varies, most traditions recognize the presence of at least five distinct layers or *subtle bodies* within the aura. Each layer possesses matter that vibrates at a certain rate and has a unique function. These subtle bodies are well defined energy fields—a series of overlapping, graduated, and interconnected layers of energy—with progressively increasing frequencies as they extend from the body. Most agree that in addition to the physical body, at least four distinct and identifiable bodies exist within the aura, including the etheric, astral (emotional), mental, and spiritual (causal). These bodies or layers are used by the highest aspects of our being as instruments of expression and action. The fields extend around the body like a rainbow.

Several studies have demonstrated young children in our culture frequently possess the innate capacity to describe certain aspects of the aura, usually vivid colors corresponding to various emotional states. Adults are most often unaware of the aura's presence. Our environment has not encouraged the development of that aspect of our being. As a collective, we've tended to focus on the material world. Because of this approach, we frequently encounter difficulties accepting and conceptualizing the spiritual portion of our being in a way that promotes the development of our innate, intuitive capacities.

The aura has been perceived to be especially prominent in persons known to express innate spiritual qualities. For example, descriptions and paintings of sacred beings in ancient Egypt, India, and Greece. Included are Isis, Osirus, Horus, Jesus, the Christ, angels, Krishna, and the Buddha. They're characteristically surrounded by luminous emanations of golden and white light.

Recently scientists have noted significant differences in aura measurements electronically obtained among healers, psychics, and yoga adepts—in comparison to people used as controls. The subjects had developed certain psychic abilities. These included telepathy (the capacity to know about events occurring at a distance), clairvoyance (the ability to see events in the future), clairaudience (the capacity to hear future events), healing, and the capacity to induce altered states. It is believed the expression of these and other intuitive abilities are facilitated by an increased sensitivity of the aura to various frequencies of a larger, universal field of energy that holds all of creation together as one.

Dating back to the time of the ancient Egyptians, people have recognized the presence of a pervasive, vitalizing, life-giving, and omnipresent field of energy throughout the universe. It links and interconnects every aspect of creation. All of creation was considered to be a part of this unifying force, which was a manifestation of the omnipresent divine creative aspect of God transcending time and space. Regardless of the various assigned names, the basic concepts and principles have essentially remained the same, intersecting a disparate group of cultures and traditions.

Today a diverse group of traditions including ancient Egyptian, contemporary African, Hindu, Chinese, Japanese, the Kahunas of the Pacific, Native Americans, and Buddhists all recognize and acknowledge the existence of a ubiquitous, divine energy. This field is believed to transcend time and space, allowing all forms of creation to exist as a part of the whole. These traditions also consider the aura to be the portion of this universal energy field primarily involved with the expression of animate life. It is through the aura that cosmic forces integrate with the individuality of each soul in an orderly fashion—imbuing the body with the radiant expression of life, vitality, and creativity.

Thousands of years ago, the Egyptians believed in *Mat*, the principle of Divine order in which the universal energy was preserved in a state of delicate harmony and order by the mutual efforts of the gods and man. From this force all of the elements of creation radiated forth. This universal energy field permeates all of life, linking and interconnecting all creation into a whole. A few millennia later the Chinese proclaimed the existence of *chi*, the pervasive vital life-giving cosmic energy present throughout the universe, while the Japanese coined the term *ki* to identify this energy. The Hindus recognized the life force as *prana*, the breath of life, maintaining for over three thousand years that breathing charges the body with prana, the breath of life.

Russian scientists recently confirmed the scientific basis of this ancient dictum, when they discerned that a portion of the oxygen we breathe is converted into a quantum of energy which increases the reserves of vital energy and charges the entire field. They found ionized air has a highly medicinal effect for many kinds of disease. Its negative ions are converted into an quanta of higher frequencies, which energizes the auric field. Nineteenth and twentieth century scientists have also assigned a variety of names to this energy, including *Orgone, Odic Force,* and *Bioplasmic energy.*

A Sufi saying tells us, "God is forever light." The universe came from and is sustained by an eternal, changeless aspect—the pure consciousness of God. The Egyptians depicted and revered the pure consciousness of God in the form of a divine fire, representing the unending flow and continuously changing nature of all things. According to their beliefs, all of creation emerged as an expression of love—divine love, the original and transcendent ultimate aspect of God's consciousness.

Throughout the ages, divine love has been viewed as the primary expression of the divine principle. The sacred fire represented the eternal, changeless essence of God. This manifestation was viewed as the unifying, life-giving force of all creation. According to ancient Egyptian, Hindu, Christian, Native American, and numerous other traditions—love was the primary underlying nature of all creation, manifesting throughout the various realms of existence. The light of God manifested from this sacred fire. Just as sunlight provides sustenance and life to the Earth, the Bible notes, "God is light. And in God there is no darkness." 1 John 1:5. The Bible also makes many references to the *light of God* as the source of healing, wisdom, compassion, and love. It tells us Jesus is *the light of the world.* Consistent with this ancient view of God and creation, a contemporary healer/priest named Akuete Durchbach of Togo, West Africa, noted the significance of this philosophy recently when he stated, "Everything comes from the flame of God!"

Remarkable findings demonstrate the truth of the ancient notion that the universe is in a web of infinitely changing and connected energetic patterns. Ancient beliefs perceived all of creation as a part of the whole and God as the pervasive, unending life force permeating every aspect of creation–the source of all life and the underlying force of the cosmos.

For our time, Einstein's theory of relativity was the first scientific premise to identify the relationship between matter and energy. He theorized that matter and energy are interchangeable and that transformation of matter to light, and vice versa, occurs at the speed of light. The ancients often considered matter to be a form of condensed light, vibrating at a frequency much slower than the speed of light. A few scientists also agree with this ancient notion viewing matter as a form of *frozen* light.

The ancient association between light and life has been upheld by scientific investigation. It is now a recognized fact that matter possesses certain characteristics similar to light. Just as light has a certain frequency, a particular matter has a certain frequency. The higher the frequency of matter, the less dense or more subtle the matter.

Therefore, the concept of solid objects is replaced by the wave-like energetic pattern of interrelationships. Elementary particles and isolated objects, as well as objective observations, have lost their true meaning. The universe is a dynamic inseparable whole, a harmonic resonance moving to the vibrations of the various aspects of divine consciousness.

Searching for the Aura

This opens a new frontier in science. "The cosmic religious force is the greatest impetuous for scientific research," said Albert Einstein. Today, a growing number of physicians and scientists now acknowledge that we possess nonphysical properties previously unrecognized and still largely unknown and uncharted.

Seeking to find the manner in which the invisible nature and the spiritual aspect of our being affects the physical body, scientists used a variety of instruments during the nineteenth and twentieth centuries. These machines have included conventionally developed ones, as well as the electronic devices created through the merging of certain Eastern and Western principles. They have studied and irrefutably documented the presence of the aura. Several of the aura's physical properties have been measured, including its electromagnetic, thermal, visual, magnetic, and electrical characteristics.

Using newly developed technology, based on esoteric principles, several independent researchers have irrevocably documented the presence of the aura. Kirlian photography, the Voll dermatron, the AMI (electroacupuncture apparatus), the Chakra Machine, and conventional electronic equipment are all instruments that lead us to a greater understanding of the nonphysical and spiritual aspects of our being, which exist beyond the physical realm. These findings confirm we are much more than a mere collection of independently functioning organs and molecules.

Scientists like Semyon Kirlian, doctors Robert Becker, Valerie Hunt, Thelma Moss, and Hiroshi Motoyama are at the cutting edge of a new era in science. Seeking to discern and reveal the seemingly unfathomable aspects of spirit and the soul, a few researchers have delved into the mysterious realms of life. Their efforts are assisting in bridging the gap between the empirical dimensions of science and the inner dimensions of expanded awareness. Their efforts attempt to correct the error of science that has failed to recognize the spiritual side of man and devoted all of its attention to the physical and organic fields.

Throughout the ages there has been a belief, for example, that at the moment of death the spirit exits (expires) from the body. Doctors have measured a thirteen ounce weight loss occurring at the moment of death. Photographs taken by Russian scientists at the time of death have shown a gradual reduction of the light radiating from a dying body. The aura becomes unstable shortly before death. A Polish physicist believes the meaning of the *Deathflash* is an emission of light at the time of death. He sees the flash as the *...electromagnetic essence of life, conscious ego emitted in space at the speed of light.* Photos of a body taken six hours after death show a markedly diminished field. Eventually there was no trace at all, only a dull glow remaining about the body. Scientists believe these photos confirm the departure of the spirit occurring at the moment of death.

In the mid 1800's William von Reichenbach noted the presence of an *odic force*, named after the *all-pervasive* Norse god Odon. This force possessed properties similar to those of an electromagnetic field with unique ones as well, within the human body. It was very similar to the ancient Chinese description of the yin and yang (negative and positive) polarities within the body.

Around the same time Dr. Walter Kilner described a glowing mist enveloping the physical form. Using colored filters and glass screens stained with dye, he noted this mist characteristically had three distinctive zones, the densest immediately adjacent to the skin. He also found that this cloud of radiation was affected by disease, mood, hypnosis, magnetism, and electricity. Kilner's extensive research led to the development of an entire system of diagnosis and treatment. His method has been used by many practitioners in Europe.

Another physician and a colleague of Freud, Dr. William Reich, described abnormalities of the flow of energy in physical disease and emotional illness. He used the psychoanalytic technique to help identify emotional blocks that corresponded with disruptions in the flow of orgone.

During the 1970's Valerie Hunt, Ph.D., a professor at UCLA, stumbled upon the presence of a high velocity, extremely small electromagnetic field. After 600 hours of using an oscilloscope to record muscle behavior in people, she found a pattern of electrical activity similar to brain waves on the surface of the body, but vibrating 800 to 2000 times faster!

Scientists have measured many of the physical qualities and characteristics of the aura. This area of investigation is truly an interface of science and spirit. It is an important cornerstone of holistic medicine. These scientific findings act as a foundation for the development of a new field of medicine known as bioenergetics medicine. It is a vitally important component of holistic medicine.

The Etheric Body

The term *etheric* is derived from ether. It was also known as the shadow among the Egyptians. It has been frequently characterized by psychics and electronic equipment as the densest component of the aura, described as a glowing white mist radiating one-half to two inches from the body. It is a definitive structure upon which the physical body is developed and connected. It is through the etheric body that energies possessing higher frequencies are slowed down to accommodate entry into the physical body. In many regards the physical and etheric bodies actually behave as a single unit.

The etheric body is the blueprint upon which the physical body develops. A few scientists speculate it represents matter from the higher frequencies of the physical realm. Acting as a pattern, it organizes matter and establishes the structure of the cells and organs. It also guides the placement of the organs during development and throughout the physical life.

It is the densest layer within the aura, located immediately adjacent to the physical body. The etheric body is structured by minute, interconnecting streams of light. It penetrates the body in the same way water fills a sponge and provides the cells and tissue with nourishment and sustenance. It acts as an interface, stepping down the energies so they are safely and adequately incorporated into the body. Within the etheric an organ exists which corresponds with organs in the physical body. This layer constantly moves and has been described as a glowing white mist about the body.

The work of several scientists today confirms the presence of the etheric and its function as a blueprint for development. During the 1930's and 1940's Dr. Harold Burr, a Yale University scientist, studied the shapes of energy fields surrounding living plants and animals. His work demonstrated the importance and the manner in which these electromagnetic fields are intimately involved with regulatory function.

Burr confirmed the presence of an electromagnetic field surrounding living organisms and plants. His

research focused on the shape of energy fields surrounding developing salamanders. He found the axis
of the energy fields aligned with the brain and spinal
cord similar to adults, and that the energy field corresponded roughly to the adult's. Burr attempted to
pinpoint the exact moment when the adult field expressed in the developing embryo. He eventually
discovered the unfertilized egg contained the adult-
like electrical axis! This information contradicted the
contemporary theory of the role genes played in
embryonic development. Other studies discovered that
seeds also possessed electromagnetic fields. He found
the seedling closely resembled the adult plant. These
and other experiments led Burr to conclude that any
growing organism is destined to follow a growth pattern generated by the electromagnetic field.

Due to either physical, emotional, or mental imbalances—a decrease in the flow of energy in the etheric
layer results in a loss of vitality. This loss weakens the
physical body and can lead to the development of
disease. These imbalances occur in the etheric before
the physical expression of disease occurs. Small, unde-
tectable changes in the physical form are also discernable in the etheric before conventional techniques can
isolate signs of disease.

Many scientific investigations with clairvoyant
diagnosis have described changes in the etheric body
occurring prior to the appearance of overt disease in
the physical body. Many psychics describe antecedent
changes in the body.

The Remarkable Achievements of Kirlian Photography

An Australian physician recently equated the
discovery of Kirlian photography on the same level as

the discovery of X-rays. It is one of the most remarkable achievements of medical instrumentation during this century. Others consider it to be even more important. This discovery challenges concepts of science that are the foundation of our perceptions of ourselves and our world. Its clinical use is undergoing evaluation at research centers in the United States, England, Russia, and West Germany. Every area of science and technology—medicine, dentistry, criminology, psychology, geology, agriculture, archeology, and forensic medicine—might benefit from the findings of Kirlian photography (also known as electrophotography and corona discharge photography). Several scientists throughout the world have had considerable success employing a variety of screening techniques to detect changes in the aura consistent with cancer, lung disease, and other diseases in early stages of development.

Perhaps the most important discovery of this century was that of Semyon Kirlian, a Russian electronics expert. In the early 1940's he accidentally discovered a form of photography that has captured an aspect of the aura. Semyon was asked by a well-known scientist to repair an instrument. When he went to pick up the unit, by chance he was permitted to observe a demonstration of a high frequency machine used for electrotherapy. During the experiment he noted a minute, but visible flash of light emanating from the subject's skin. Other scientists conducting similar experiments had also noted sparks radiating from the body. These findings were mentioned in numerous reports, without noting their source or significance.

Semyon wondered if this light could be photographed. He immediately set out to do so. Working with his wife, Valentina, and experimenting primarily on himself, the Kirlians developed equipment that could photograph the body's light emanations. It was done by virtue of electrically grounded objects in the presence of high energy electrical fields. Using a spark generator oscillator, and generating in the range of 75,000 to 200,000 cycles per second, they demonstrated that spark discharges created in the field caused the object to radiate visible light.

This revealed brilliant light—a kaleidoscope of streams of bright scintillating colors in varying hues of blue, purple, white, and orange emanating from living organisms. They also learned inanimate objects express light, but not in the same dramatic fashion. Variables were found to affect the photographs. But under controlled circumstances many investigators have succeeded in obtaining pertinent information concerning the organism's biological state and disease propensity.

Monitoring a leaf at different stages of the life cycle, Kirlian found changes in the heralded death. A famous Russian scientist invited him to analyze two practically identical leaves from the same species of plant. Repeated photographs from one plant consistently expressed vibrant spherical flares that were dramatically different from the other's dark geometric colors. No adjustment could alter the pictures, leading Semyon to believe the technique was inconsistent and unreliable.

The Russian scientist returned and was amazed by the findings. He explained to a distraught Semyon that the second leaf was from a tree afflicted with a serious disease. The disease had not yet expressed any physical manifestations. These and photographs of other animate objects consistently demonstrated that distortions and abnormalities occur in the energy field before disease manifests in the physical form.

The aura also has intricately organized networks that unify the various layers and allow the exchange of energies. The etheric body penetrates the physical body through specific passageways. It is interconnected to the physical body through several channels which allow the dynamic interchange of energies. These networks act in a manner similar to the nervous system in our physical body.

The Body's Meridians

Until the latter half of this century Western science had little knowledge of these systems. The Chinese system of acupuncture has been used for almost four thousand years. It is a therapy that uses needle insertion at specific points on the body's surface known as *meridians*. The meridians are circuits which act as channels allowing the entry of *chi*, the life force into the body.

According to ancient Oriental theory, twelve pairs of meridian channels exist within the body. Traditional acupuncture theory believes life energy flows regularly through the body along channels entering and leaving the body at specific points. Each meridian pair governs the flow of chi for a particular organ system. To a certain degree, these pairs correspond with the physical organs. For example, there are splenic, heart, liver, and kidney meridians. Imbalances and blockages of the system often precede the development of physical disease. Early detection and correction of the energetic imbalances can prevent such development. Acupuncture (needle insertion at specific meridian points) can facilitate the healing of existing physical disease. In the West, the meridians were never believed to actually exist, until the work of a Korean scientist proved there were physical forms corresponding with the meridians.

Professor Kim Bong Han conducted a series of studies using rabbits to determine the presence of the acupuncture meridians. Injecting a radioactive substance into surrounding tissue and analyzing the results using a specialized technique (microautoradiography), he found the radioactive substance was actively taken up by a microscopic duct-like tubule system. These structures followed the pathways of classical acupuncture meridians. Concentrations of the radioactive substance in the tissue of the surrounding area were negligible. And when it was deliberately injected into a blood vessel in a nearby vein, none was detected in the meridian network. This finding suggested that the meridian system was independent of the vascular network.

The tubular system is divided into a superficial and deep system. Kim also found these ductile systems reached the nuclei of the cell. He further discovered higher concentration of compounds that are extremely important to the function of cells—including DNA, RNA, amino acids, hyaluronic acid, sixteen types of free nucleotides, adrenaline, corticosteroids, estrogen, and other hormonal substances—in levels much higher from those ordinarily contained in the bloodstream.

In one study he severed the meridian supplying a frog's liver and studied microscopic changes in the liver tissue. Shortly after severing the meridian, the liver cells became swollen and very turbid. Within three days, the entire liver began to slowly die.

Kim concluded that the meridian system not only inter-linked within itself, but appeared to interconnect with all cell nuclei of the tissue. He also learned that in the embryonic chick, meridian ducts were formed within fifteen hours of conception—before the even most rudimentary organs were formed. This led him to theorize that the meridians exert an influence upon the spatial organization, migration, development, arrangement, and specialization of the cells of the internal organs during embryonic development and throughout life. More recent work by French researchers and others have confirmed Kim's findings in humans.

Other studies have demonstrated differences in the electrical, electromagnetic, and electronographic qualities of the acupuncture points. This is discussed in a later chapter.

Seven Major Chakras

Within the human aura other networks exist which also facilitate the channeling and exchange of energies with the universal energy system. Both ancient Hindus and Egyptians described an energy system within the layers of the human energy system. These energy centers are most frequently termed *chakras*, the Sanskrit term for wheels, because they resemble whirling centers of energy. Esoteric literature is replete with descriptions of the chakras.

The seven major chakras are located along the spinal column. Each one is associated with a group of nerves and a major endocrine gland. It is also associated with a particular type of psychic functioning . . . and possesses its own optical, auditory, and vibrational frequency. These energy centers—in addition to acting as channels—are also transformers of the universal energies, accommodating their entry into the cells and tissues in a manner similar to the meridian network. The specifically targeted areas are the major endocrine glands that are necessary for the maintenance of physiologic function.

According to ancient scriptures, each chakra is reflective of the state of the tissues in the immediately adjacent areas, and reflects the attunement of all aspects of being. The primary chakras originate at the level of the etheric body and extend into the other layers.

In another experiment—conducted by Dr. Hunt in conjunction with Rev. Rosalyn Bruyer—a well-known California psychic was asked to comment on the changes in the color she noted in the subjects aura while he was being rolfed (Rolfing is structural integration of the body, a manipulative procedure developed by Ida Rolf.). Concurrently the aura was electronically monitored. Mathematical analysis of the data measured revealed Reverend Bruyer's findings were exactly the same.

Using specialized equipment to measure the steady, low-voltage wave forms, four of the twenty-four subjects were monitored while being rolfed over 10 sessions observed by an aura reader. Electrodes were placed at eight traditional chakra locations and acupuncture sites: Pilot studies had previously established recording sites for major chakra regions where artifacts were minimal.

The data was intercepted by a four-channel EMG instrument and recorded on one track of a two-track tape recorder. At the same time Bruyere recorded on the audio rack a description of the color, size, and activity of the auric fields of subjects and rolfers. Using a second microphone, subjects described their spontaneous experiences and images during rolfing. Doctor Hunt monitored all incoming data by earphones and by two-oscilloscopes in a glass-enclosed room. The reader was questioned using an independent audio system without receiving any information.

The electrical impulses correlated reliably with colors reported by the reader. The colors often, but not always, corresponded with metaphysical descriptions. The energy seemed to move in two directions: towards disorder or order. The energy coincides with emotional states, imagery, interpersonal relationships, and physical body plasticity.

According to Hunt, because it documents previously unknown aspects of our being, these findings are significant because they document the presence of certain previously unrecognized nonphysical structures.

The Chakra Instrument was created by Dr. Hiroshi Motoyama to detect the energy generated in the body, and emitted from it, in terms of various physical variables. It detects minute energetic alterations (electromagnetic and optical) on the surface of the subject's skin, using computer analysis of the immediate environment. His findings were similar to those of Dr. Hunt's in terms of identifying differences in energetic patterns at the traditional chakra sites. Further, he learned that people with innate psychic abilities were capable of controlling the energy flow through the centers, to a certain extent.

Several ancient sources believe the major chakras have a particular frequency, color, sound, structure, and psychospiritual function. These centers mediate the levels of biological, emotional, psychological, and spiritual health; they facilitate the flow of cosmic energy into the physical form. The major chakras are listed in the Appendices.

If healing was as it seemed, the harmonizing of the disquieted, a balancing of energies to bring about peace...then healing is clearly not limited to even the visible.

—*Stephen Levine*

Chapter 7

The Path To Rejuvenation

Many of my patients and workshop participants have asked me one basic question, "How do I begin to heal myself? I don't know how to start, can you help me?"

I've heard this question from those in the throes of serious and sometimes life-threatening disease, from some in the midst of emotional despair, from others seeking a fuller way of living. They attempt to leave behind stress-ridden lifestyles and unhealthy behavior patterns. They seek peace, healing, and new meaning in their lives—a reprise from the terrain of despair within their beings.

People have often been led to believe that a doctor, therapist, or healer is someone who can do for them what they cannot do for themselves. This is not true. Every person has the capacity to heal whatever needs to be healed. *Healers* are at most facilitators. Ironically, I've seen people who are beginning to heal and have a significant transformation in their lives, abruptly stop their therapy.

Where does the path of healing—the road to health, well-being and transformation—begin? The way of healing is an intrinsic and inseparable part of life. The potential for healing is everywhere! It is a precious part of our inalienable birthright. It is the process of expressing our innate and intrinsic wholeness of the spirit, allowing it to issue forth into our body and mind. The path of healing is not a course of extremes. It is one of awareness and balance. There's no mystical formula that can or will magically release us from our responsibility and our suffering. Each of us must confront the areas of disharmony and disease in our lives. An honest assessment of ourselves can lead to the process of transformation. One that approaches the seemingly fragmented aspects of our being, piercing the cloud of the unknowing, and consciously returning us to our innate wholeness. Healing leads us to peace, harmony, fulfillment, and purpose.

All the techniques and principles discussed in this book stem from the underlying reality that ultimately all healing comes from God. It manifests through our essence—the soul, a core of divine love. We are created in the image of God, the image of love. The essence of our being is a place where peace, joy, mercy, grace, and compassion abide. At our core, we are essentially good, loving, and lovable—regardless of what the world tells us.

Many names have been given to this essence: the soul, the Divine spark, God, the Christ consciousness, the light, Buddha. In spite of the diversity of names, in terms of interpretation it is essentially the same. Our essence is connected to all things, to all of life and its underlying source.

The path of healing is from its core, leading us to wholeness and unity. It is inextricably linked to healing the physical, emotional, mental, and spiritual discord that marks our life. Peace of mind, self-acceptance, and knowledge of God comes from living in tune with one's inner self and experiencing the spirit within.

Healing is unique for each of us. For a few it comes quickly, occurring spontaneously. Most commonly it takes months, years, sometimes decades. Even when it does happen suddenly, it is only the beginning—an initiating event of sorts. Usually it is subtle, yet equally profound in the long run. Each type of healing reflects the continuous unfolding of the spirit.

Healing fosters honesty in perceptions of our emotions. It brings an increasing state of clarity and evolving awareness of the oneness and unity of life within ourselves and all of creation. It facilitates the resolution of denial, breaks down behaviors that have prevented an honest assessment and transformation of old wounds, and soothes fear.

It allows us to heal old emotional wounds, to confront the disparaging memories of the past that have haunted our being. The process fosters a growing awareness of honesty, forgiveness, and completion. It is a process where the newness of life, the refreshing fragrance of love, permeates. This leads to peace, contentment, and healing.

Most commonly there is a sincere desire to be healed. This is often prompted by the presence of a life-threatening disease, which leads to the beginning of the conscious process.

Because the mind and body are integral, the vast majority (if not all) of illness carries significant psychosomatic components where emotions have contributed to its development and progressions. I believe every disease has an underlying emotional, mental, psychological, or spiritual dimension—one that either directly or indirectly affects the course. Yet illness and disease don't have to be viewed in a negative, despairing light. They can be considered as a friend, an instructor, a blessing rather than as a punishment. Disease often captures our attention—in a way nothing else could—causing us to focus our awareness on the prevailing imbalances and disharmony in our being.

We are not ordained to have a life filled with pain and conflict. Yet journeying through this life, we have all experienced pain, both physical and emotional. Life is difficult. The ancients always recognized this reality. It is often shadowed by chaos, conflict, and confusion—both internal and external.

There is an inherent mystery circumscribing life. The difficulties and challenges are a part of that mystery. All the great religions speak of the inherent and inseparable difficulties of life, from which no one is exempt.

Jung once said neurosis is always a substitute for legitimate suffering. I believe that notion can be extended to include physical disease as well. Our avoidance of pain and anguish—rather than resolving and healing the emotional wounds that we have experienced—can assist in the development of disease.

Many believe the pervasive spiritual discord and detachment from love existing in our world stems from the inability to express our highest purpose in every level of our being. Our spirits long for expression, recognition, and light in our daily lives. This requires re-harnessing of our purpose. Maladies of the spirit do not stem from an essence that is pure, unencumbered love.

I believe the divine longing to allow the spirit to manifest, is an expression of the life force dwelling in all of us. The spirit offers the possibility of a clearer knowledge of the self and a broader understanding of the world in which we live. It also offers healing for those seeking to resolve disease and imbalance. It allows our awareness to pierce the veil of unknowing, to bring to the surface the ancient wounds that have shadowed our lives and eclipsed our spirits.

The gift is that disease has the potential to resolve the attendant physical, emotional, and spiritual components within our being. Healing most commonly comes at a time of upheaval or a time of searching for a greater understanding of life, for the spirit and healer within.

In the midst of pain and anguish I've seen many touch upon something whole, a part of their being they'd never known before. Watching the blossoms of being emerge from the murky waters of pain and regret is a privilege to behold. This expression of wholeness and inner peace is often hidden beneath the underlying anguish and pain that has become central to our lives. We suffer when we fail to see our connection with our spirit, our essence, our oneness with God, others, and all of life.

Members of our society tend to be more distanced from their emotions than other peoples. We are often unaware. We fail to recognize what is going on internally, even when there is severe pain and deep despair.

We've been led to believe the physical world is the ultimate reality, that our accomplishments in it are the source of happiness and well-being. Therefore we don't pay attention to our inner life. Because we are out of touch with our spirits, we lack meaning and purpose. We seek to avoid pain—rather than acknowledge, then resolve it.

It is often said that we live in an addictive society, one that promotes unhealthy activities and destructive relationships. I believe this is prompting our collective healing crisis. It is bringing to the surface the disruptive and diseased aspects of our society. Our cravings, which lead to addictive and other destructive and disruptive behaviors, are part of our search—attempting to soothe the inner longings of the spirit and desperate emptiness. We suffer when we fail to see our connection with our spirit, our oneness with God and all of life.

As a society, we have bought into the promise of material consumption and external acquisitions as the way to happiness and satisfaction. Now we are beginning to see these things in a different light, recognizing life suffers from imbalance when the focus is on the external. Harmony and peace rests in striking a balance between the various aspects and expressions of our being.

The happiest people I've met were those who lived in accordance with their spirit. They lived in the moment, honestly acknowledging all aspects of their being. This potent aspect of life is always present, only appearing to elude us—hiding beneath the pain and anguish, the disharmonies that have accumulated over a lifetime. The process of healing is facilitated not necessarily from knowledge and understanding, but through experiencing a connection with the whole.

Some of the most powerful and dramatic occurrences of healing I've witnessed were preceded by emotional breaks in the armor of despair, bringing hidden memories of pain and anguish to the surface and allowing them to be healed. Healing frequently is accompanied by a removal of the blocks, patterns, and emotional wounds that prevent its expression. The more we resist the more it hurts. The more we deny, the more we attract.

The search for harmony and this sense of self—the fragmented parts of being and the outer world—is the foundation, the primary focus, of our spiritual quest. It ultimately results in the discovery that the source of our greatest wisdom lies within. We may learn from many sources, but ultimately we must learn to trust our own innate wisdom—the guidance God has given us.

I am always amazed by the resiliency and fortitude of children. It seems the younger they are, the greater access they have to their inner healing. It could be due to their lack of emotional baggage. This awareness and recognition leads us to the path of healing.

In allowing disease to be embraced, an untapped reservoir of healing is called forth from the spirit. The patients most successful in the process I've seen are usually those who come to a graceful, loving acceptance of disease— ending the war of pain and conflict and resting in a place of tolerant allowing. The contemporary medical model frequently overlooks these components, continuing to view the body as a machine. This fosters inherent limitations to the view of the dysfunctioning whole.

The Road to Self-Love

One of the most important components of the foundation of healing is self-love and acceptance. I've heard patients ask, "How do I begin to love myself? What do you mean? I feel so unworthy? I've known how to love others, but not myself. Where do I start?"

Many of us have grown up in environments that were not conducive to self-love. Our families were dysfunctional and the environments were often not conducive to self-love. Many of us did not receive the nurturing and affection that is vital for healthy development. Beyond our physical needs, we all need love—especially during our childhood. Ultimately self-love leads to a broader, more expansive acceptance of life. Self-love is flexible, giving, compassionate, and understanding. One of the easiest ways to begin to love yourself is to begin to pay attention to yourself—

to thoughts, emotions, and feelings. We often criticize more than praise. We play the old tapes of the disciplinarian: don't do this and don't do that.

Just do a simple exercise. Spend ten to fifteen minutes each day, when you can't be distracted by the demands of daily life, and quietly reflect on *you*. Your thoughts, feelings, experiences. Give yourself undivided attention. I advise patients to begin to focus on the nurturing aspect, the side that is free of guilt and criticism. Participate in daily nurturing of the self.

True and honest self-love is not narcissistic. In our culture narcissism and self-love are often confused. True love of self is neither selfish or greedy. It sees the self as part of the whole, and is the personalized, individualized expression of agape—unconditional, divine love. Love without condition is divine. It is a radiant force and is part of the greater, universal, divine order of love. Narcissism is reflective of the lack of conscious love. It is demanding, egocentric, immature, devouring. True self-love is ever present, we only need to remove the disharmony that prevents its expression.

Arrogance and selfishness are outward manifestations of fear and insecurity. A secure soul is an open, loving one. Narcissism seeks to soothe the pain, but it is a poor substitute. It can lead to destructive, addictive behaviors. It seeks from the external world; nurturing love comes from the core.

To me, love—unconditional agape, as termed by the Greeks—is the source of all other loves. Self-love is the individualized, personalized expression of agape. We truly cannot love others without loving ourselves as well.

One of the easiest ways to love oneself is to start paying attention. Tune in to your thoughts, emotions, feelings, and fluctuations in your body. We often criticize ourselves more than we praise. Because we do not love ourselves, we feel unlovable. Positive attitudes assist the process of healing, as long as they are authentically positive.

The search for this sense of self—for personal harmony and power—is a spiritual journey. It leads to finding our greatest truth, one that rests within our very core. Because our primary nature is spirit, life offers the ultimate opportunity of spiritual growth and development. This is the essence of our spiritual odyssey called life. There is an element of mystery inherent to our spirit. The essential part of our being brings to us a sense of wholeness and contentment. It brings peace, transforming our lives into the rich state of being they were intended to be. Living moment to moment in its awareness, removing the shadow of denial and the clouds of despair, it gives way to a wisdom that comes from the holy divine, quiet core.

The search for this sense of self—for harmony with the inner being and a sense of personal power as a part of our spiritual journey—leads us to find our greatest truth and purpose. Ultimately we must learn to trust our inner guidance. It comes from living in tune with our inner self.

Unfortunately, more often than not, we are trained by the world to ignore our own guidance and to focus on its criteria. However, when we learn to trust and accept our inner guidance it leads us to our highest good. It fosters self-awareness, acceptance, forgiveness, understanding, and resolution, increasing the expression of wholeness. Awareness brings to the surface the issues that require immediate attention. In quiet meditation I've seen many old, unhealed wounds emerge through years of silence.

Self-Love Allows
the Expression of Our Wholeness

Nothing has to be different for us to be whole. It is a matter of change. It has to do with loving acceptance, change in perspectives; not in positional changes. This doesn't mean everything is coming up roses. Difficulties persist, sometimes even become greater. It is the way we handle them, not their absence, that is the mark of spiritual growth. To be whole is to be complete, to be all encompassing. Transformation and healing softens our anger and allows us to be more loving. To be whole is to take ourselves within through the eyes of love.

We are responsible. We make choices, conscious and unconscious ones in terms of how we will respond to any situation. There is no need for guilt or blame, only to understand and to heal.

One of the most powerful examples of transformation I've witnessed was the healing of one of my dearest friends. Judith had a difficult childhood, growing up in an alcoholic home. She was an artist, realtor, and teacher.

Several years ago, while living in the Bay area and attending a school on healing arts, she became very ill. She spiked fevers to 107—accompanied by excruciating headaches, drowsiness, and severe weakness. She was found to have Rocky Mountain Spotted Fever. During the first few weeks of the illness she decided against hospitalization. Judith proceeded to try to heal herself with vitamins, nutrition, herbs, meditations, visualizations, and affirmations. This was an extremely difficult period. In addition to her illness she had very little money, couldn't work, and her sister suddenly committed suicide.

While focusing on visualizations and affirmations, she experienced a transforming shift in consciousness. "I learned the power of positive thinking, but that it is a tenuous process," she explained. "I was positive for so long, refusing to acknowledge my emotional pain, that I never completely healed. Finally when I just allowed myself to accept the totality of my being, then I was healed completely."

After several months, the disease subsided and she began to regain her strength. She resumed her work while studying a variety of healing techniques. For several years during the 1980's she counseled people with AIDS. She has an integrative approach that takes into consideration nutritional deficiencies and psycho-spiritual components.

The basis of many emotional problems stems from the perceptions we have. We see ourselves as unlovable and intrinsically defective. Frequently I've heard my patients speak in different ways of how unlovable they are.

Letting go of the anger, pain, and distress is most difficult and challenging. Sometimes it seems impossible. But it is not. Letting go and allowing is the most difficult.

In our society we often frame our attempts to heal in a fighting, aggressive sense. It is important to accept, rather than reject, what will allow the dissipation. The unhealed needs to be embraced, and the healing called forth. The most successful patients I've seen, in terms of healing, are those who find a place of graceful inner acceptance of all aspects of their being and experience.

Faith, Forgiveness, and Fortitude

My experiences with people in the midst of confronting and curing a vast array of illnesses and diseases showed me many common qualities and characteristics in those who experienced healing. They commonly share three qualities during the process: faith, forgiveness, and fortitude.

One of my favorite Bible stories is about a woman with an issue of blood. She was afflicted with this disease for more than twelve years; no doctor could help relieve her symptoms. Then she heard of Jesus, of the miraculous healings, and decided she did not want his attention...only to touch the hem of his garment. When she did this, she was healed instantaneously. Until she touched him Jesus was not aware of her presence. But he knew someone had touched him in a different way. "Who touched me?" he asked. The woman was afraid to make herself known to him, but did. He told her to be happy; it was her faith, not he, that had made her whole.

Because faith engenders hope, it is the fuel that gives life to the will. According to the Bible, "Faith is the substance of things hoped for in the evidence of things not seen." It transcends belief and is reflective of an intuitive knowing of the truth that persists in the face of contradictory evidence. Faith transcends the realities of our existence. It cultivates hope and a spirit of renewal. It shows whether or not what we say we believe is actually what we believe.

The capacity to express faith in varying degrees is probably the most common quality I have seen patients express. I believe faith stimulates physiological changes that promote healing. Yet it must be distinguished from false hope. Faith emerges from the spirit, while false hope resides in the purview of the ego.

Because faith is born of the spirit, it is accepting and does not deny reality. It merely sees beyond it. Faith survives and is a manifestation of the will to live. Many times during the years of my medical practice, I've had the privilege of treating patients who possessed unbelievable amounts of faith in the midst of seemingly hopeless situations.

Mrs. Georgeton was such a patient. She was a middle-aged woman with the most severe case of pulmonary hypertension (high blood pressure in the lungs) that I've ever seen. The cause was unknown. She'd been afflicted with it for several years and had slowly deteriorated, though to the surprise of all of her physicians she hadn't died. One of the pulmonary specialists on her case told us she had the highest levels of hypertension he'd ever seen in twenty years of practicing.

One day while attending to her she said to me, "Dr. Ferguson, I know all of you think I should be dead, because my disease is so bad. But I know I'm not going to die anytime soon."

"Mrs. Georgeton, you certainly have surprised us, because you've done so well with your disease. It's really amazing to me. But how do you know you're not going to die yet?" I asked.

"I'm not going to die at least until after Christmas. I have too much to do. I have a grandbaby that's due in November, six months from now. Christmas is my favorite holiday and I'd like very much to see all of my family together one more time during the holidays. Plus my husband is slowly accepting the fact that I'm dying. If I hold on just a little longer, he'll be far better after I'm gone." Every morning I'd go to the ward expecting to be told she had passed on.

She was eventually discharged from the hospital on oxygen. Mrs. Georgeton lived for six and a half months longer than anyone ever dreamed she could. She died quietly in her sleep shortly after the beginning of the new year.

Forgiveness is one of the most challenging components of healing. It is not an endorsement of wrongdoing, but an act of releasing the pain and hurt through love. In order to heal we must forgive, because healing and anger cannot occupy the same space as love quietly engenders forgiveness. It is an exercise of releasing the past pains, wounds, and anguish that have facilitated disease. As in love, we must first forgive ourselves for our transgressions. We must give up the shadows of past unhealed wounds. No one is exempt. We cannot truly love ourselves without forgiving. Once we begin to forgive ourselves we can forgive others.

Forgiveness allows us to move on, releasing the ties that have bound us to our past. These old unresolved wounds impede and interfere, circumventing our healing. Often we can be more forgiving of others than we are of ourselves.

How do we begin to forgive? How do we forgive those who have caused us great pain? It isn't easy; but it is imperative. As in the case of self-love, we must first forgive ourselves for our own transgressions. Forgiveness aids in the process of halting self-abuse and hatred. We must forgive ourselves and others in order to be whole and healed. When we open our hearts the first areas that need to be forgiven the most are usually not the wrongdoings that come to mind, but the deeper hidden transgressions that have lurked in the recesses of the unconscious mind. Because they are so severe, they tend to surface gradually. Type "A" personalities have a higher risk of heart attacks because of hostility and unresolved anger, say researchers—not because of their competitive, driven personalities.

Many of us have made our way through life avoiding and suppressing our pain, rather than confronting it. Breakthroughs occur after months or years of therapy when painful memories come to the surface. When those wounds are healed, forgiving transformations occur. We often feel less slighted, less inadequate, more loving.

I had a patient, John, a young man in his early twenties who was prompted to see me because of a severe case of ulcers. His pain was minimally improved by medication and he refused to have surgery. Over several months of approaching his illness holistically there were symptomatic improvements, but no significant abatement occurred.

He was very resistant to dealing with his emotions and wanted to limit the focus of therapy to his physical symptoms. That is until one session, when during meditation, old memories suddenly rushed to the surface. He spontaneously recalled several episodes of severe abuse during his early childhood that his father had inflicted upon him. He was not conscious of these experiences, although he was aware of the deep resentment and anger he felt for his father.

During the months that followed, John began to consciously confront and heal the old wounds and pain in concert with confronting his father and attempting to heal their relationship. While his father initially denied ever abusing him, he finally admitted it. John's ulcer began to improve during the period of emotional healing. His symptoms went away and he no longer needed to take the medication for pain.

Fortitude allows us to face life with confidence. It is a resilient determination that springs forth from spirit, not circumstances. It prevents us from succumbing to the ups and downs, the tragic episodes of life, and is the substance of the will to live.

I am always amazed by the resiliency and fortitude of children. It seems the younger they are, the greater access they have to healing. One of the most moving experiences occurred during my final year in medical school. Yolanda was a little baby girl whose story has vibrantly remained with me for over a decade. During the seventh month of pregnancy, her mother suddenly went into active labor. At that time—the mid 1970's—there was no medication to reverse the process. Before she was born, the obstetrician knew the chances of the baby surviving were virtually nonexistent.

Yolanda was born, a very tiny and severely premature baby. She weighed less than two and a half pounds. At the time of birth the only signs of life she exhibited were very faint heartbeats and what is termed *agonal* respirations that occurred occasionally. Her breathing pattern consisted of shallow, erratic grunts. In light of her smallness and the fact no baby her size had ever survived, the attending obstetrician informed her parents that their little baby girl was born dead.

After the delivery, the staff followed routine procedure, notifying the pathology department that her remains needed to be picked up for an autopsy. She remained alone in the delivery room for several hours. In that cold, dark room—unbeknownst to anyone—Yolanda clung to life.

When the technician arrived hours later that night to collect her body, he was shocked to find a breathing baby. He notified the doctors on call in the hospital's intensive care nursery. In light of her severe prematurity and extremely small size the decision was made not to vigorously resuscitate her. The doctors were certain she would not live through the night, especially since several critical hours had lapsed between the moment of her birth and her arrival to the unit. During the night, she was given only minimal life support, oxygen through a hood, instead of the usual full ventilatory support with a respirator.

The next morning she was still alive—and kicking, much to the surprise and shock of the staff in the nursery! Since her vital signs had slightly improved and stabilized throughout the night, a decision was made concerning her care—as well as what to tell her parents since they were not aware their little girl was alive.

The obstetrician that delivered her and the pediatrician in charge of the nursery visited the mother's room that morning. Together they told the parents their little girl was alive by virtue of *an act of God.* They also gave them very little realistic hope in terms of her survival, anticipating that she'd live no longer than a few more hours or days. The doctors told the parents not to expect to ever take their baby home from the hospital.

In spite of everyone's appropriate reservations concerning Yolanda's survival, after the decision was made to treat her, no holds were barred. She was placed on the complete life support that she'd been denied for several hours—including a respirator, heart monitor, umbilical artery catheter, and appropriate medication.

Throughout the first few weeks of her little life, Yolanda was never more than a breath away from death. Her vital signs were tenuous at best. One complication ensued after another, arising with unbelievable regularity. Yet she simply refused to die. Over the weeks and months that followed, she very slowly began to improve, valiantly fighting off one life-threatening infection after another. She conquered multiple brain hemorrhages, jaundice, repeated blood transfusions, and lung damage due to prolonged exposure to high oxygen levels. Her spirit never allowed death's ever-present shadow to cover her tiny body and enormous will to live.

Her improvements grew beyond the minute, incremental ones that initially occurred. She began to gain more weight, strengthening her reserves. She slowly began to respond to her environment, smiling at her parents and nurses, suckling and cooing—but at a much slower pace in comparison to normal babies. Gradually she started to grasp the fingers of her nurses. There was a moment of celebration in the nursery on the day she grasped a small toy in her hand. The infections ceased—the internal bleeding in her brain stopped—the transfusions were no longer needed. And with great difficulty she was tenaciously weaned from the respirator that had acted as her lungs for so many months.

I was privileged to be on call the Sunday afternoon that Yolanda was discharged from the hospital. After a six-month battle, she defied the odds—as well as her doctors' realistically grim predictions—and went home with her parents. For me, it was the highlight of my years in medical school—a thrilling moment that will live with me for the rest of my days. It was touching, emotional, and uniquely rewarding to see that little baby girl who had in six months faced and overcome a seemingly infinite number of insurmountable obstacles.

She has given me courage, faith, strength, and a profound appreciation of how indomitable the human spirit is. In moments of my weakness, I often think about Yolanda. Sometimes I wonder where she is and how life is treating her. Yolanda is just one of the patients who clearly showed me the powerful role the will to live plays in healing.

> Within our hands resides the capacity to heal.
> —*Anonymous*

Chapter 8

The Healing Touch
—Miracle of the Ages

Several years ago I had an experience I'm certain dramatically influenced the course of my entire life both personally and professionally. My receptionist's husband, David, came to the office to see me because of an injury he'd sustained nine days earlier during a skiing trip. While skiing on a downhill course, he fell and injured his right knee.

The next morning he woke up to find his knee had developed mild swelling and bruising with severe, unremitting pain. After a week the swelling and bruising went away; but the pain persisted, interfering with David's walking and his ability to carry out his job. When I examined the knee, I found tenderness and mild swelling. X-rays of the knee were normal. With the diagnosis of a right knee contusion I gave him the routine therapy of crutches, an ace bandage, and a mild anti-inflammatory medication. I instructed him to return to the office for a follow-up visit in one week.

Two weeks later he brought his son to the office for treatment of a sore throat. While examining Chris, I remembered David hadn't returned for his follow-up visit. Because he didn't have to pay for my services, I thought this was strange. I asked, "Why didn't you

come back to the office last week?" He replied, "I
didn't have to come back!"

"What do you mean you didn't have to return?" I
asked. "I didn't have to come back because you healed
me! What did you do to me? After you examined me,
that night the pain began to go away. The next morning I woke up, all of the swelling and pain had disap-
peared. Do you practice magic or something?"

"No, I don't," I replied. "I don't know what happened." After they left the office, Pat, our office
receptionist, said to me, "Dr. Ferguson, I've been
meaning to tell you what David said. He was so excited—he said you healed him. 'What did she do to me?'
he wanted know. He feels you are more than a doctor."

I was completely unprepared for this experience,
confused yet excited. I knew something was happening
to me. I'd been praying and asking for a sign of the
direction my path should take. And this experience
was a significant one. I knew it was evidence of a
healing force moving through me and an indication of
things to come. And yet at that same moment I knew
I was merely an instrument, a part of a process that
was far greater than myself. I was humbled to have
the opportunity to participate in this. Fortunately the
event happened at a time when I was seeking.

The healing touch is one of the most ancient and
commonly used forms of therapy known to exist. The
annals of recorded history are filled with accounts of
its use. It has been associated with spiritual healers,
mystics, and healers of all types. The Bible and other
sacred texts also record healings stimulated by touch.
Probably best known in our culture are the reported
healings of Jesus of Nazareth who is credited with
giving sight to the blind and making the lame walk.
According to the *Ebers Papyrus*, a medical text found

in the nineteenth century from ancient Egypt, the use of laying on of hands was part of their holistic approach to healing nearly five thousand years ago. King Olaf of Norway was also known to possess the healing touch, as were the Roman emperors Vespasian and Hadrian.

The primary characteristic has been the belief in a universal, omnipresent power linked to an infinite source of healing—known as God, Allah, the Source, or the Great Spirit. The therapeutic use of hands is a universal act.

Today laying on of hands (LOOH) is practiced throughout every part of the world, in a variety of forms. It is called many different names—Reiki, Johrei, therapeutic touch, magnetic healing, psychic healing, psychic surgery, Mahikari, healing touch, Midas touch, and others. These different types are all variants of the same form, adapted to meet the particular needs of the culture.

It is one of the most common forms of healing and has been modified and integrated into a diverse group of traditions and cultures. Thousands of doctors, nurses, and health professionals in the U.S. and throughout the world use it as an integral part of their practice. For over a decade in Great Britain, healers have been working side by side with doctors. Studies of LOOH healing capacity have been conducted in several American hospitals and universities.

What Is Laying on of Hands?

Quite simply LOOH is a process of transferring energies using the hands. In this universal energy transfer, the *healer* acts as a conduit. The transfer of these energies stimulates the removal of energetic blocks, abnormal patterns, and other irregularities. It promotes and harmonizes normal flow within the aura—which in turn fosters and stimulates balance within the physical, etheric, emotional, mental, spiritual, and physical realms augmenting the natural healing process.

The healer facilitates the process of self-healing and can impact locally and at a distance. Numerous scientific studies, including Kirlian photography and other electronic measurements, have documented these changes. Laying on of hands, like other healing techniques, helps to foster the process of innate wholeness. It is essentially a process of becoming integrated and balanced with our essence. It is different for different people. It not only occurs on a physical level, but on an emotional and spiritual one as well.

On the nonphysical levels of being, disease and illness manifest as an imbalance of energies. Prior to the development of physical and psychological disease, changes occur within the aura preventing the normal flow that maintains the body's innate balance. The objective of any healing therapy is to reestablish this normal flow of energies. It is not dependent on either a religious context or the patient's faith in the healer. Laying on of hands assists the natural healing process in a profound and moving way.

It is a process of altering the aura. It can be conducted within any context or framework—the physical, mental, or spiritual. Until recently many scientists and laypersons believed if healing actually occurred, it was simply due to the healer's power of suggestion. Science has shed a lot of light on this phenomena, documenting the presence and transfer of measurable energies within the electromagnetic realm. Astounding discoveries have been made concerning the nature of the healing capacity as a part of untapped human potential.

In the course of my spiritual quest, while researching and reading about a variety of spiritual and metaphysical topics, I was particularly drawn to the laying on of hands. The books that captured my attention more than others were those on healing, especially the laying on of hands.

I read about many healers including *Mystic with Healing Hands*, a biography of Olga Worrall. She and her husband Ambrose were two well-known healers in the United States during the 1950's and 1960's. For many years they provided spiritual healing through the laying on of hands and prayer to a countless number of diseased and afflicted persons, in addition to subjecting themselves to numerous scientific experiments that documented their capacities.

I read about Doctor Brugh Joy's spiritual quest. Brugh left behind his successful medical practice in Southern California for a spiritual quest that led him to places throughout the world. His book was especially comforting to me to know I was not alone, but in the company of scientifically trained women and men who were seeking a greater understanding of the mysteries of life.

Finding the Right Teacher

During my residency, about four years before my experience with David, I met a woman who subsequently became a good friend. Roberta Glenn was a well known psychic in the Chicago area. On several occasions Roberta told me that I was a *healer*. At the time I was not impressed by her statements; I felt being a physician was healing work. As time passed I began to comprehend the full meaning of her prophecies. It was after my experience with David that I came to understand in a different light what *healing* and *healer* meant.

A few days after my experiences with David, I knew it was time to find a teacher, someone to guide this path of healing. The books I'd read were helpful, informative, and comforting; but something was missing. I needed a personal instructor.

I prayed, asking God to send to me a teacher and guide. A week or so later I stumbled upon a copy of a catalogue for the Oasis Center in Chicago. I'd never heard of the center before and was surprised to find their catalogue in a record store, of all places. It is a center with a twenty-year history of conducting training programs for the advancement of human growth on the emotional, intellectual, and spiritual levels. They sponsor workshops and courses on Gestalt therapy, massage therapy, and traditional forms of healing including Native American Shamanism, Kahunas, and Buddhism.

Reading through the catalogue, I found an introductory seminar on the laying on of hands that was very interesting to me. It was entitled, "Opening to Our Light," conducted by Judith Citrin. When I read Judith's biography I knew I'd found my teacher. She had been a well-known international artist. A near death experience prompted many changes in her life, personally and professionally. She subsequently ended her artistic career and became what she calls a *transformational therapist.*

Her work consists of an intuitive utilization of counseling, dream analysis, laying on of hands, imagery, meditations, and visualizations—all to promote healing and transformation of the emotional, spiritual, and mental levels. Judith had studied with several doctors including Brugh Joy, Richard Moss, and

Stanslov Grof. All of them have utilized various healing techniques like imagery, prayer, meditations, visualizations, laying on of hands, and rebirthing. She'd also received instructions from several Reiki masters. Reiki is an ancient Japanese form of healing.

At the request of a surgeon friend of hers, Judith performed laying on of hands at a local private hospital in the Chicago area. They wanted to see if it would have any effect on hospitalized terminal cancer patients who were resistant to pain medication. Her work significantly reduced the need for powerful narcotics such as Demerol or Morphine. The patients reported a significant reduction in the level of pain and were able to sleep better at night. And during abdominal surgery she channelled energy through a patient's body. This decreased pain, hospitalization time, and the need for drugs.

Because my schedule prevented me from attending her workshop, I contacted Judith through the center. She called and we talked briefly about her work and my desire to find a teacher. We agreed to meet at her home a couple of weeks later. I was excited. I knew beyond intellectual understanding that she was the person I'd been searching for. And I also knew we would do many things together in the months and years to come.

On the day of our meeting, while standing on her porch, I realized I'd seen the front of her home in a dream a few weeks earlier. Our meeting seemed more of a reunion than a first get together. A sense of familiarity and love that usually takes months and even years to develop, spontaneously occurred the moment we met. Judith was filled with a radiant light. I liked her immediately. I told her of my experience with David and of my interest in finding someone to teach me how to heal through LOOH.

In addition to over a decade of teaching and facilitating healing, Judith has trained many including doctors, nurses, and therapists and other health professionals. She agreed to become my *teacher.* We decided to meet at her home on a regular basis for a six week period of training.

About ten days before our scheduled sessions, I was involved in an automobile accident. My car was struck while turning at an intersection. Because I wasn't wearing a seat belt, my face struck the steering wheel. I suffered a mild concussion. The next morning I awoke with a continuous high-pitched ringing in my ears. After a few days of this unremitting ringing, I decided to contact an ear, nose, and throat specialist. A friend of mine strongly recommended I see one of her colleagues. Unfortunately, I couldn't reach him to make an immediate appointment. I decided to call Judith instead and have a session of laying on of hands with her.

She saw me a couple of days later and did LOOH while guiding me through a few meditations that included visualizing white light entering my body. As she touched different parts, I felt warm, electrical vibrations flowing from her hands and through my body.

By the time the session was over I experienced a state of peace, relaxation, and well-being unlike any other I'd ever felt. The ringing in my ears did improve, but it persisted. The next morning when I awoke, however, it was gone. It never returned again.

During the next six weeks Judith and I met in the evenings at her home. The training consisted of guided meditations and visualizations, learning how to channel energies through the chakras and hands, sending and receiving light through the body, and increasing aura sensitivity and awareness.

I began to understand that in very real and discernable ways, we are more—much more—than our physical bodies. During my training with Judith I became aware of the presence of the aura. I discovered how to detect imbalances, blocks, and irregularities—and how to remove them.

Slowly I recognized a profound truth: the body holds within it the innate capacity to heal itself. I realized one form of therapy, like one medication, doesn't work in every case. There are many components to the healing process—spirit, emotions, lifestyle, behavior, and nutrition all play a part. I've seen patients improve with a variety of treatments.

Now I was faced with the challenge of assimilating this new knowingness into my daily professional life. Because I practiced with a group of physicians, I decided against incorporating laying on of hands into the practice, since it was not a part of standard accepted medical procedures. At that point I wasn't comfortable with the idea of incorporating it into my own practice. My scientifically trained mind continued to ask questions. I decided to initially limit the use of this treatment to family and friends. I found it to be extremely helpful for some individuals, while in others its effects were minimal.

A part of me was very uncomfortable because this process extended beyond the boundaries of my beliefs. I did not know how to resolve this disparity within myself. As the weeks progressed, I began to feel a sense of dichotomy developing in my life. The differences in my approach to patients in my conventional practice, in comparison to those I worked with in a holistic fashion, was troubling to me. My scientific background would not allow me to openly accept. I constantly asked myself, "What's going on? Is this real or am I crazy?"

This time was important. It was a period of questioning and reconciling the seeming differences, allowing for growth and integration. I could not blindly accept what I had read and even experienced as true. It had to sink in. I had to reorder the manner in which I perceived the world.

What I was doing was to become a larger and more significant part of my healing practice. I did not know how to resolve this seeming conflict and disparity within myself. I felt there was a vast difference—a rivalry even—between orthodox Western medicine and the ancient healing techniques I'd become involved with. Many months would pass before I realized *the disparity resides with our perceptions and beliefs*, and not intrinsically with the different therapies.

It was not easy for me to accept what I was experiencing. Years of training had left an indelible imprint upon my mind. I frequently told myself I was crazy, that I had lost touch with reality. Yet a part of me knew something important was happening. Upon learning this new skill, I was confronted with the dilemma of what I was to do with it.

My experience with laying on of hands eventually became extensive and diverse. I probably use it more frequently than any other therapy in my holistic practice. Regardless of the disease, I've seen it consistently promote a deep and profound state of relaxation, plus improved clinical symptoms of physical and emotional disease. It has promoted improvement of hepatitis, AIDS, cancer, liver disease, menstrual disorders, menopause, decreased joint swelling, asthma, and such other disorders as obsessive compulsive or addictive behaviors, diabetes, fractures, and migraines.

In a few instances I've seen physical and emotional healings occur spontaneously. This is an exception and not the rule, according to a variety of healers. Usually there is improvement, a gradual improvement and often resolution of physical and/or psychological symptoms. Sometimes the symptoms spontaneously disappear, occasionally they get worse—prompting a healing crisis. Most commonly they improve gradually.

Mrs. Williams was a participant in one of my workshops on healing. She'd suffered severe back pain due to an arthritic condition for several years. The pain was continuous and virtually unresponsive to medication. While her symptoms were minimally improved, she suffered side effects of the medication. About a week after the workshop she called me to let me know that the morning after the workshop she awoke free of pain. For a week she couldn't believe that her arthritis had improved so significantly. Neither could her doctor, who ran tests and found the physical signs of the disease, including improvement of X-ray findings, were perplexing to him.

For many years now, healing through the use of laying on of hands has been a part of my life. More so than any other aspect of my healing practice and the path I chose to take, it has profoundly affected my beliefs and perceptions of who I am and who we are. It has vividly brought into my life the spiritual aspect of being, in a real and palpable manner. It has molded the life I chose to lead.

First, because I am so actively involved, it has allowed me to see the integrity of being, more so than any other healing modality. It has demonstrated how we are integral beings and linked to all of life.

Because it facilitates the healing process through repairing the aura, I've seen deep hidden emotions surface from particular areas that seemingly acted like magnets, attracting disease and illnesses. I've seen how integral the body actually is when emotions are mended, how disease and illness begin to improve and dissipate.

Because of the way I was trained, initially I had a routine, a set way of performing this technique. As time progressed, I came to see all that was necessary was for me to be open to whatever I needed to do at the time—to stop my mind from overworking and be an open conduit—to allow the universe to use me. It is a powerful manifestation of the way the unseen forces impact upon us if we are open and accessible.

Laying on of hands has profoundly touched my life. It has reshaped the way I view healing and illness, and humbled my view of myself as a healer. I know I am merely acting as a tool. I am extremely grateful for the opportunity to serve in this capacity. These experiences have shown the way the spirit affects matter.

I eventually began to conduct seminars in the Chicago and midwest region. Many of the patients participating in these seminars were persons seeking a greater understanding of healing. Some reported dramatic healings—the sudden and spontaneous disappearance of diseases and illnesses—while others noted mild improvements. Most commonly the changes were subtle, occurring over a period of time.

During the years I came to see that the underlying presence and expression of love was the key to healing. Sometimes a simple act of compassion and affection was more effective in the healing process than the laying on of hands itself.

The concepts of modern science have not expanded to encompass the actuality of healings that have been consistently reported throughout the ages and in all parts of the world. Laying on of hands has been unacceptable and misunderstood. Its been erroneously branded as unscientific magic.

Science still doesn't know exactly how it works. It can measure certain physical parameters. Despite this resistance, healing using this technique continues to be reported at an accelerated rate.

The investigations of scientists throughout the world have shed light on this phenomena, documenting the presence and transfer of measurable, high frequency energies within the electromagnetic realm. They have made important discoveries concerning the true nature of this particular healing phenomena.

During the last half of the twentieth century, many remarkable and astounding discoveries have been made concerning the nature of these healing energies. Numerous scientists, healers, and health professionals have documented the healing effect of laying on of hands. They include Olga and Ambrose Worrall, Brugh Joy, M.D., Dolores Krieger, R.N. and Ph.D., Elmer Green, M.D., and Thelma Moss, Ph.D.

Olga and Ambrose Worrall were two of the best known healers in the nation during the 1950's and 1960's. Over the years they successfully treated thousands with diseases *incurable* in the eyes of medical science. As their notoriety grew, doctors throughout the U.S. made referrals to them. The Worralls were voluntarily subjected to a wide range of scientific studies, including distant healing, Kirlian photography, and measurements of their *psychic ability* that confirmed their healing abilities and scientific studies. Tests even verified their psychic ability at a distance.

Using Kirlian photography, Dr. Thelma Moss, a medical psychologist at UCLA's Neuropsychiatric Institute, photographed a leaf of a plant as it appeared in its natural state. The leaf was severely damaged, removed from the plant, and cut. A photo was taken of a bleeding gap over the damaged area. Olga held her hand over the leaf and administered healing to it. The next photo showed dramatic changes. The photo taken after healing revealed a reorganization within the damaged area. It was filled in with brightness.

In another series of experiments, Sister Justa Smith had Olga hold and heal several objects—including damaged enzymes, distilled water, whole blood, and serum—to see if her touch had any effect. Kirlian photos of the specimens taken before and after, showed clearly visible change within the aura.

There are a few difficulties and limitations in the case of studying healing. An ill person is not a lab experiment. There are many variables involved that cannot be exactly replicated. Furthermore, patients tend to seek healers as a last resort: rarely do they come untouched by medical science. Even where proof seems obvious, only a few doctors have been willing to substantiate the evidence.

Biochemist Brad Gill of Montreal's McGill University was sure the scientific method in properly controlled lab conditions could knowledgeably answer the questions of certain aspects of spiritual healing. In a study funded by the Parapsychology Foundation, which he carefully designed and painstakingly controlled, he attempted to answer certain questions. His results were significant. They opened the minds of doubters and detractors alike. Using animals and plants to eliminate the placebo effect, his results were observable and duplicated by other scientists.

His studies evaluated the physical aspects of healing. He acknowledged and believed in the therapeutic powers of spiritual healers. He suspected there were certain factors operating that were difficult to discern and confirm. His experiments successfully demonstrated the truly energetic phenomena and aspect of the healing touch.

Gill teamed up with Oskar Estebany, a well-known healer and former soldier in the Polish army, who had successfully treated many diseases. They used a strain of mice with an increased incidence of goiters in the thyroid gland. This strain was selected because of Estabany's previous success treating humans with this disease.

The mice were placed on a diet that made them more likely to develop goiters, a diet deficient in iodine, necessary for thyroid functioning. They were also given a thyroid hormone that acted as a blocking agent. All of the mice were initially held to distinguish the calm ones from the nervous ones. To control for human heat a control group was placed in cages wrapped by electrothermal tape to simulate the warmth of human hands. A third group was held by nonhealers. The experiment lasted for forty days. Compared to the control animals, the mice receiving the healing touch from Estebany show a significantly slower rate of goiter development.

Additionally, cotton and wool pieces were placed in the cage floors of mice. Material charged with the energy from healers was left with the mice for an hour in the morning and afternoon. Similar charged pieces of cotton and wool were placed in the cage of control mice on the same diet. The mice in the group receiving the charged fabric showed a slower rate of goiter formation, preventing the development of disease.

In another study of the effects of laying on of hands on wound healing, an area of skin was surgically removed from forty-eight mice. The mice were evenly divided into three groups. One group was exposed to laying on of hands, another group was treated with artificial heat (the same temperature as the hand for the same amount of time), while the third group served as the control. After eleven days the wounds of the group exposed to laying on of hands were significantly smaller than those in the other two groups.

In another experiment three hundred mice were wounded and divided into three groups according to weight, age, general health, and wound size. One group was exposed to the healer, another to medical students without known healing abilities. On the fifteenth and sixteenth days of the experiments, the average surface area of the wounds of the group exposed to the healer were significantly smaller.

Justa Smith, another scientist at McGill University, demonstrated the effects of energies emanating from healer's hands on test tubes of enzymes. They acted similar to high intensity magnetic field energies. Injured enzymes were reorganized, promoting order. She found the energies acted in a scientific way and had the capacity to alter the behavior of the enzymes in an intelligent, organized, and cohesive manner.

Hans Engel, M.D., and chief of staff at Holy Cross Hospital in Mission Hills, California, conducted an eighteen month healing experiment with Dr. Thelma Moss. He successfully treated several patients with diseases such as Bell's palsy, deafness caused by meningitis, and spinal abscess. In 1974 he experienced the sudden remission of a supposedly terminal case of advanced lymphatic sarcoma. After that time he noticed his innate capacity manifesting in other patients as well.

Dr. Ben Leichtling of the University of Colorado School of Medicine noted in his experiments, a small but significant change in cell culture growth patterns occurred when using healers.

Also at the University of Colorado, John Zimmerman, M.D. and an assistant professor of psychiatry, has adapted a machine used to measure the brain's magnetic field to monitor the entire body. When a trained practitioner of therapeutic touch attempted to heal an eye, elbow, or knee, he observed distinct changes in the patient's field. Signals up to several hundred times larger than background noise appear while the healer works. The investigations of others have documented several physiologic changes within the human body and animals during the laying on of hands, including brain wave changes.

Qi Gong, the Chinese form of healing that manipulates vital energies, has been shown to cause changes in the brain stem and cortex, as well as decreasing the growth rate of 60% of laboratory bacteria and a 30% decrease in the growth rate of cervical cancer cells.

Therapeutic Touch

More so than any other individual, Dolores Krieger—a tenured professor at America's largest school of nursing, the New York University Graduate School of Nursing—has affected the way laying on of hands is perceived and accepted as a healing therapy. She became interested in the healing effect when she was a nurse assisting in experimental studies of the purported healing abilities of Oskar Estebany.

Nearly twenty years ago she developed a nonreligious, secular form of laying on of hands known as *therapeutic touch.* Her work and that of her students has provided the greatest amount of credibility to this form of healing. She has brought it into the mainstream of medical practice. She researched the literature on touch and concluded, "The touch in which I was interested was not simple physiological touch, but rather touch which conveyed an attempt to help or to heal."

Therapeutic touch is a derivative of the laying on of hands in which the therapist uses hands to assist and to heal. She and several of her students have conducted extensive research on the physiological effects of therapeutic touch. She worked from a basic assumption that we are open systems of energy fields and exquisitely sensitive to energy. She saw the act of healing as a channeling of vital energy from an individual with an overabundance to the ill person.

Man is an open system—always engaged in the transfer of energy, in a state of continuous change on many levels, always flowing in, through, and out. On the physical level it occurs by an act of electron transfer resonance and the recipient reestablishing the vitality of the flow of this open system. The patient heals his or herself—as a resonant effect of the system.

Over 20,000 doctors, nurses, and other health professionals throughout the world have been taught how to perform this simple form of therapy as an adjunct and complement to conventional medical treatment. The Order of Nurses in Quebec voted recently to accept therapeutic touch as a bona fide skill for 50,000 nurses. In 1987 Kreiger was awarded the National League of Nurses prestigious Martha E. Rogers Award.

Some of the studies have been funded by the government. Krieger's study, "Therapeutic Touch During Childbirth Preparation by the Lamaze Method," and "Therapeutic Touch and its Relation to Marital Satisfaction and State of Anxiety of the Married Couple," were funded by the Department of Health and Human Resources. Also, Dr. Janet Quinn's study, "The Effects of Therapeutic Touch on Anxiety in Pre-operative Open Heart Patients," was funded by the National Institute of Health, Center for Nursing Research.

Also, therapeutic touch in nurseries has been shown to increase survival rate, significantly increasing the hemoglobin level and reducing anxiety in cardiac patients. It occurred to her that an appropriate variable hemoglobin might be affected. It is the component of the red blood cells that carries oxygen and is sensitive to oxygen's uptake. Grad's experiments at McGill had shown an increase in plants affected by the healer. She was intrigued by the similarities in structure and function between hemoglobin and chlorophyll. Krieger theorized that the healing energies probably had a similar impact upon the hemoglobin molecule. The hemoglobin structural features are the most clearly understood human protein, an index of the body's basic metabolism.

The experiment controlled for all variables including age, sex, drugs, vitamins, nutritional intakes, biorhythm, and smoking. Krieger directed 32 nurses treating 64 patients in metropolitan hospitals and health care centers in New York. To eliminate bias, lab technicians were not informed of the study. Uniform blood analysis equipment was used. According to her, the probability of the shift in hemoglobin values being a chance occurrence was approximately one in a thousand. The experiment confirmed the findings of a 1971-1973 project.

Studies of Krieger during a healing session found she goes into a state of synchronous, rapid beta activity, when focusing her attention in a healing meditation and using the laying on of hands. Eric Pepper, of Albany Hospital in California and President of the Biofeedback Research Society, and Sonisa Ancoli, of the Langley-Porter Neuropsychiatric Institute, confirmed Krieger's studies. They noted three earlier reports had found similar rhythms in advanced mediators.

The Power of Prayer

Prayer has been one of the major healing practices throughout the ages. Scientific studies continue to provide exciting insight into the mysteries of such healing. A study conducted by a professor at the University of California, San Francisco, showed the effects of prayer on patients in a coronary care unit at San Francisco General Hospital.

A randomized, double blind study of 393 patients was conducted by three cardiologists. One hundred ninety-two were prayed for by people recruited by Dr. Randy Byrd. Those praying were Protestants, Catholics, and Jews around the country. They were given the patient's name, diagnosis, and condition—and asked to pray each day. Every patient had five to seven people praying for him or her.

In spite of the two group's similarities, there were significantly different outcomes. The prayed for subjects experienced fewer complications in three major areas: they required less antibiotics (3 compared to 16), experienced decreased incidence of pulmonary edema (6 compared to 18), and none of the prayed for needed to be placed on a respirator, while 12 of the others did. Based on these findings, the physicians concluded prayer is effective and beneficial.

Other doctors throughout the country agree prayer is beneficial. Dr. John Merriman, chief of staff at Doctors Medical Center in Tulsa, Oklahoma stated, "I believe that patients named in prayer do better." While Arthur Kennel, an assistant professor of medicine at Mayo Medical School, said the study gave scientific credibility to his own observations. "I pray for my own patients and I feel my prayers benefit them."

Olga and Ambrose Worrall participated in a study conducted by Dr. Robert Miller of Atlanta, Georgia that attempted to ascertain the effect of prayer at a distance on a growing plant. Dr. Miller monitored the growth of a rye grass plant in his Atlanta laboratory for several weeks. The growth rated was measured by an electrical transducer connected to the blade, to an accuracy of 1.0 milliliters per hour.

The growth was stabilized at a rate of 6.0 milliliters per hour for several days. At 8:00 P.M. one evening he called the Worralls at their home in Baltimore requesting they pray for the plant's growth at 9:00 that evening. They were asked to visualize the plant growing vigorously under ideal conditions. The following morning the tracings were analyzed from the tracing on a strip-chart recorder.

Prior to the beginning of their prayer, the growth rate was 6.25 cubic millimeters per hour. At precisely 9:00 P.M., the tracing began to deviate upwards. By 8:00 the following morning, the growth rate was 52.5 cubic millimeters per hour—an increase of 830%. The growth was charted for forty-eight more hours. During that time the growth did decline, but it remained greater than the original rate.

Throughout the experiment the conditions were unchanged and untampered. There were no known factors which could have caused such a dramatic increase in the growth rate of the plant. The findings were accepted as documentation of the fact that Olga and Ambrose, six hundred miles away, were able to stimulate the plant's growth by an eight-fold increase through praying for less than five minutes. The power of prayer exemplified!

Drugs are not always necessary. Belief in recovery is.

—*Norman Cousins*

Chapter 9

The Healing Mind

The air was filled with a palpable electricity, a sense of escalating anticipation. Akuete Durchbach, a small, humble middle-aged African man—who has a well-deserved reputation throughout West Africa, Europe, and parts of the United States for his enormous healing abilities—emerged from a small hut in his compound and stood briefly before his American guests.

In 1987 a group of sixty Americans had travelled to Lome, Togo, a small country located on the coast of West Africa. They went to study and learn about traditional African spirituality and healing. They were about to witness an ancient fire ceremony, among the few Westerners who had been made privy to the ancient African spiritual traditions that have frequently been misrepresented and distorted in the West.

A group of fire dancers called forth the fire spirit to consume a pile of green wood that had been cut earlier that day for the ceremony. Before their eyes, Akuete stepped into the fire. He remained in it for several minutes. Then he calmly emerged from the fire as if he'd just taken a stroll around the block. Neither his body nor his clothes were harmed!

Akuete's feat is just one example of the tremendous expression of mind and body that has been known and utilized in various parts of the world. Throughout the ages adepts, healers, gurus, and followers of a variety of disciplines have performed startling feats while in altered states of consciousness. Fire-walking, and other amazing manipulations of the physical body, occur in Africa, the South Pacific, Eastern Europe, Indonesia, and the USSR. While in the West these practices have remained cloaked in mystery, they have flourished in other cultures for centuries. Throughout time the vast majority of the world's spiritual traditions and healing systems have viewed the mind and body as one integral unit and considered the mind to be the doorway to a higher consciousness and a greater awareness of God, the essence of all things. The body was believed to reflect the state of mind and acted as an individual unit. Because of our focus on measurable parameters, our belief system has limited the way we perceive our physical world. Consequently we are amazed at what others can do.

For centuries the healing powers of the mind have been harnessed through a variety of techniques, including meditation, visualization, affirmations, and eliciting faith and hope. Throughout the world harnessing the powers of the mind was an important aspect of these techniques, utilized in most of the world's healing traditions, and was used until 1650 A.D. in the West.

In general the physical changes are secondary to the achieved altered states of consciousness. It is believed that these states of expanded consciousness foster spiritual growth and development. They demonstrate the enormous powers the mind exerts upon the physical form, as well as the effect of mind over matter. During the 1970's and 1980's these remarkable physical changes were studied by several scientists who attempted to understand the phenomena of altered states and the impact upon the body's physiology.

For ages most of the rest of the world has known that the mind can intervene and direct any physiologic function. Human beings have an innate biological awareness of their physical state, down to the level of the single cell. In the West, science is beginning to explore and document seemingly unlimited powers of the mind. Since the 1960's when transcendental meditation was introduced to the general public, there has been growing interest and use of meditation for spiritual growth and healing. Previously the role of the healing powers of the mind has been overlooked, discarded, minimized, and often ridiculed by modern medicine. In the West the mind was perceived as a totally separate and distinctive entity from the body. The obvious impact of the mind on the body was vehemently denied.

Today a growing number of doctors, nurses, scientists, and other health professionals are seeking to learn more about the interface and unity of mind/body. This is reflected by the increasing research interest in this area and the burgeoning acceptance and use of healing techniques that involve the mind. Many are recommending the use of a variety of meditative practices for a number of diseases. Therapists use it for emotional healing. Even the AMA recommends that meditation be used as the first line of therapy in the case of mild hypertension.

To unleash the healing powers of the mind in my holistic practice, I use several healing techniques—including meditation, imagery and affirmations, or the art of positive thinking—on a daily basis. Meditation is used as an adjunctive therapy in the treatment of every case. As far as I'm concerned there is a place for these healing tools in *every* disease. Others have also used them in a diverse range of diseases, including cancer, ulcers, hypertension, burnout, AIDS, fibroids, and diabetes mellitus. I have found that these techniques can be used in any clinical setting with significant results. Harnessing our natural healing capacities is one of the most powerful healing tools there is.

A young woman in her mid-twenties, came to see me several years ago because she wanted to cure a chronic infection involving her lymph glands. June was quite different from most of the people I see. She had a high-powered sales position in a family business and was not receptive to a holistic approach. She had the mistaken notion that I could simply evoke the healing powers to dissolve the swollen gland and that would be it.

She was only interested in using meditation, not any other techniques. Setting aside all other considerations, we did a guided meditation. Like most patients I've used meditation with, she initially experienced a deep and profound state of rest and relaxation. During the course of her therapy, June very slowly began to change the world she was accustomed to. Her first step was to end what she perceived to be an unhealthy relationship with her boyfriend. She moved into a new apartment and also worked on improving her relationship with her parents. Although she elected not to leave her job, June successfully negotiated decreasing her responsibilities and her work load. This gave her more time to pursue other interests. Consequently, her disease has remained in remission.

Medicine's Skewed View of the Placebo Effect

Placebo is derived from the Latin word meaning *I shall please.* No active or curative ingredient is involved. It is given only to calm the patient and usually elicits a beneficial effect. A good example of medicine's skewed view of the mind is its perceptions and reactions to the placebo effect.

For years the placebo effect has been cloaked in misunderstanding and mystery. Until recently doctors have had a rudimentary understanding and awareness of the powerful effect the mind exerts upon the body. While testing the usefulness of new drugs they found the placebo elicited the same effect as the drug. A patient is given an inactive, inert substance that has no pharmacologic impact, but is quite effective in terms of evoking a healing response and a significant amount of improvement.

I remember the attending physician who described it to us in a lecture titled The Placebo Effect—we have but a rudimentary understanding of this phenomena. Historically, it has not been well received. Most doctors don't understand the significance of the placebo effect.

The placebo effect was viewed in a narrow, myopic way. It did not take into consideration the holistic role the mind plays, but saw the influence of the mind upon the body in a limited way that interfered with science's purist approach to investigation. Doctors often looked upon it with annoyance; it interfered with the scientific pursuits of the purists.

I personally found the whole notion of the placebo effect quite remarkable. There are reports of patients responding positively to drugs based on initial reports—then subsequently *not* responding once the drug was found ineffective.

Studies today show patients can be told a substance is inert, but in spite of this knowledge, a healing response can still be elicited when the placebo is taken. By the same token, a placebo can have harmful effects. The placebo clearly demonstrates how effective beliefs are in terms of profoundly impacting an individual's physiology and evoking a healing response. The mind reacts to what it believes; what you believe, you experience. Belief in healing can exert a key role in generating physiologic responses that are healing and harmonious...or disruptive and disease causing. Beliefs can dramatically alter the physical body.

Thoughts also impact the aura. Kirlian photography shows demonstrable changes in the electrical discharge pattern with varying thoughts. Loving thoughts of God have a distinctively different pattern in comparison to sporadic irregular patterns of anger.

We also know that verbalizing a belief, even if one doesn't truly believe it, impacts upon the body. Everything we say, think, and do contributes to the overall balance and state of our being. Affirmations, positive statements said in a repetitive fashion, can also assist the healing process and have been used by scores of nontraditional healers in our society.

Today there's an ongoing debate concerning the degree of that influence. On one hand traditional medicine based on Descartes' theory says the mind and body are separate—while on the other hand a trendy New Age notion says we create our own reality. Notable metaphysicians and healers claim we are 100% responsible for everything in our lives. This view and the old world scientific view is diametrically opposed.

Some have taken an extreme interpretation, a belief we are personally responsible on a conscious or unconscious level for everything that happens to us. I've seen many feel guilty about not *healing* themselves. Several patients have come to me, with a deep sense of guilt and shame, wondering what they didn't do correctly because they didn't will themselves back to health. They felt shame because their bodies weren't healed, in spite of their efforts. People feel guilty and unworthy when physical healing doesn't occur. On the other hand, I've seen persons who felt no responsibility whatsoever in terms of their afflictions. We honestly don't know all of the reasons and causes of disease.

Both are extreme attitudes; one fosters guilt while the other supports victimization. The notion that the disease just happened is as debilitating as the belief that everything in our lives is within the realm of our external control. We must recognize there are some forces beyond our control. I believe it is part of the natural evolution to take such an extreme position, in light of the pendulum swinging.

I think for the majority of us the truth falls somewhere in the middle. My experience and observations lead me to conclude that the mind does exert an influence upon the body and the course of disease and health. But this response is variable at different times and unique to each and everyone of us. I do not believe that it is the ultimate determinant in the resolution of physical symptoms and disease.

Because we live in a world that focuses on the material aspects, we tend to equate healing only with the disappearance of any signs and symptoms of disease. But the role the mind plays in healing is not limited to that. Healing involves all elements of our being. Sometimes we can be healed emotionally, yet disease progresses because it is time for the individual to move on to another plane of existence. Also the disappearance of disease does not necessarily mean healing in terms of the essential nature of wholeness.

I've seen many subject their bodies in vain to a variety of painful procedures and techniques in the name of healing. For some, no matter what they try, healing does not occur. These are not failures. In my opinion, they are simply ready to move on to another life, another aspect of life, another place.

There is a story in India about a man going to see a saint, asking for healing of his dying friend. The yogi ignored the man's requests and was quite irritated by his persistence. After several attempts, he told the man to leave his friend alone. There was nothing he could do to keep his friend on the planet; he needed to move on to another place that was his destiny.

The Attitude of Healing

Belief, thoughts, and emotions all impact upon our physiology and contribute to the creation of our experience. I've personally observed several patients defy the current understanding of medical science. I've seen them refuse to accept their terminal prognosis and fight back with a tenacious fortitude and gallant determination. They simply refuse to die—not only adults, but children also.

We know personal beliefs shape our perceptions and our view of reality. Without a doubt the mind and body reacts to what one believes. If you believe you're going to die, that belief will assist the process in a variable way. It will increase your chances of dying. Conversely, you will increase your chances of healing if you believe you will be healed. But that doesn't necessarily insure healing or death will occur. It will, however, affect the physiology and can support such thoughts and emotions.

In terms of physiologic responses there is little difference if what is perceived is far greater than what actually exists. For example, dramatic physiologic responses are known to occur during hypnosis. Studies have shown the power of suggestion in this state. A person told his body is being touched by a hot coal develops a burn, in spite of the fact the object was an ice cube! And just the opposite has happened also.

Initially AIDS was believed to be 100% fatal. This death sentence, I am certain, contributed to the high incidence of fatality. Today many are defying death and living years beyond their expectancy. I've treated several people with various degrees and stages of AIDS who have lived far longer than ever expected. I'm amazed by their resiliency and progress as they move daily a world shadowed by constant reminders of pending death.

We know our perceptions of control impact upon the body. Our emotions consciously and unconsciously shape the perceptions. If we live in fear, then we see a fearful world. Studies have shown humans and animals exposed to uncontrollable situations are considerably more susceptible to developing disease. Rats exposed to inescapable electric shocks were less likely than others to reject implanted tumors. Sixty-three percent who could escape shocks rejected the tumor, while only 27% of those who couldn't escape did. Of those not exposed to shocks, 54% were rejected.

But humans are different from animals. We make choices in terms of how we respond emotionally, in comparison to the automatic response of animals. The flight or fight response, as mentioned earlier, is determined by our perceptions.

In the workplace we believe upper level management is at greatest risk for the development of disease. But studies show those workers who have less control are more at risk. Because we focus on the phenomenal world and controlling it in every way possible, it is little surprise to see the untold effects controlling the external world has upon our bodies.

Ancient and contemporary spiritual teachers insist one of the true paths to spiritual growth and development rests in surrendering to external influences. Allowing them, rather than manipulating and seeking to change them, moves oneself beyond the seemingly endless dichotomy of good and bad, right and wrong, joy and pain. It heads us toward the unchanging state of rest in the will of God. Surrendering leads to a diminished need to control, increases flexibility to adapt to the unavoidable and painful aspects of life, strengthens the body, and increases resistance to disease.

A decreased need to control and flexibility in a changing environment increases resistance to disease. Positive mental states seem to bear favorably on health and longevity. One study found joy, mental resilience, and vigor were the second strongest predictors of survival. They were only secondary to the length of the patient's disease-free period.

We know long-term frustration and chronic hopelessness leads to disease because these emotions increase susceptibility through lowering resistance. We also know that flexibility to change increases resistance to disease and capacity for health and that the deepest relaxation is being one with yourself and at home in your body. Attitudes toward stress are determinants more so than the situation itself. When the source of stress is prolonged or undefined or when several sources exist concurrently, it is much more difficult for an individual to return to a normal state.

Attitude has a potent effect on our capacity to maintain health. A defiant fighting spirit can increase longevity. Empowerment, some control regardless of how small, is an important psychological consideration. Positive mental states seem to bear favorably on health and longevity. One study found job, mental resilience, and vigor were the second strongest predictors of survival after being disease-free.

An optimistic outlook accepts change as a part of life. It is something that usually requires a considerable amount of time and patience to develop. A positive attitude, in order for it to be truly healing, must be genuine. As part of the wave of New Age thought, I've seen many people in a state of denial of anything that is deemed negative. The truly healing attitude embraces every emotion and appropriately faces them.

The healing attitude of belief, a hope for improvement, fortifies the process of healing. There is a biology and physiology induced by hope that can assist the healing process. It is a determination without desperation—a commitment to heal and live life to the fullest. Healing is not about the avoidance of death, which is an inevitable part of life, but about the full exploration of life—living each passing moment in complete awareness.

When we believe we can be healed we help to activate the mechanisms that foster healing—on every level, not just physical. Probably the most remarkable healings I have seen happened on the emotional and spiritual level.

Healing techniques such as meditations, affirmations, imagery, biofeedback, autogenic training as well as a positive, healing life-affirming attitude assists the process. In the next section we will take a look at some of the healing techniques I use most frequently in my holistic practice.

Using Meditation Techniques

Dr. Keith Wallace and Herbert Benson, research scientists at Harvard University, documented a state of profound rest induced in persons practicing transcendental meditation. Dr. Benson, a research cardiologist, was prompted by Wallace, who was his assistant at the time, to practice transcendental meditation. Wallace convinced Benson to study mediators to see if there were any measurable physiologic changes occurring during meditation. His findings were reported in prestigious medical journals. They discovered the ability to relax through meditation exerted the same state of relaxation Hesse had discovered in animals decades earlier. In humans this state had a healing and calming effect upon the body.

This relaxed state is governed by a particular area in the hypothalamus, which has been shown to be elicited by meditation. Physiological responses include a decrease in oxygen consumption, heart and respiratory rates, blood pressure, and muscle tension. Brain wave patterns change from the alert beta state to a relaxed alpha rhythm also occur. Blood flow is diverted from muscles to the brain. A warm feeling, a restful state of heightened awareness takes place. In stressful situations the heart, lungs, and blood pressure rate all increase. Meditative states induce exactly the opposite—a decrease in the respiratory, heart, and blood pressure rates. Relaxation occurs on many levels and in a variety of ways and can be stimulated using a multitude of techniques that are essentially interchangeable: hypnosis, muscle relaxation, meditation, controlled breathing, and biofeedback. Meditation doesn't necessarily have to be tied to any religious practice. Through relaxing the body and other physiologic changes, meditation facilitates coping and the innate healing process.

Transcendental meditation not only offers protection from disease, it also slows aging. Studies showed the length of time practicing correlated with the years of reduction in aging. Long-term meditation affects several key hormones, including those produced by the pituitary glands. Benefits are regulated by changes in brain chemicals, decreasing the aging process.

A Harvard study found meditation led to more refined mental control, less emotional involvement with thoughts, greater discriminative capacities, greater insight, and refined mental control.

Meditation has been used in a variety of settings—in hospitals, the corporate world, prisons, for world peace in reducing conflict, violence, and strife in war-torn areas throughout the world. There is a meditation room in the Pentagon, and a form of meditation has officially made its way into the United States military training programs as a method of coping with stress. U.S. Navy Human Resources Management has used the relaxation response, without ideology, and had a favorable response.

While Folsom Prison and several others have used this technique, studies found self-image improves and significant enhancement in mental health occurs. For three months 26 prisoners and 30 controls were monitored in terms of anxiety, neuroticism, hostility, self-concept, aggressive behavior, resting blood pressure, sleep patterns, and pulse rate. Those who meditated showed significant improvements.

It has been used in the treatment of alcoholics as an adjunct to conventional therapy in an attempt to learn new coping mechanisms. It's also been discovered that combining meditation with another therapy, such as imagery, works better than one process alone.

The techniques appear to have a synergistic effect upon the healing process.

Meditation appears to dramatically change the physiologic response to fire and cold. Fire-walking has been an ancient healing and religious rite in Africa, the South Pacific, India, Indonesia, Eastern Europe, the USSR, and Greece. Many Americans have walked across hot beds of coal with no injuries aside from occasional superficial blistering.

Greek fire-walkers who were evaluated were found to have increased corona discharge during the rite. This was marked by streams and sparks and significant brain wave changes. It is believed by the scientists evaluating the fire-walkers that the self-regulation and control over bodily functions, the act of *mind over matter,* was enhanced by long rituals and a deep spiritual belief. Faith assisted them in successfully walking on fire. Sometimes walkers were burned if they were less certain about their ability to walk.

Imagery as an Influential Tool

Imagery is another ancient healing technique that has recently emerged as a powerful tool. It is a technique that has been used throughout the world since the time of the Egyptians. It was practiced in the Americas, other parts of Africa, Tibet, China, India, and in Europe until the mid-seventh century. It induces physiological response and changes. It has been used in conjunction with such therapies as meditation and prayer.

Imagery is the act of the mind making pictures. When we think of imagery one usually conjures up visual images, but it includes all sorts of sensations—physical and auditory. Mental imagery includes more than just the ability to visualize. It's internalized experience of emotions, words, sounds, kinesthetic, even subtle body sensations. Carl Jung called imagery the directed waking dream, active imagination, and guided affective imagery. We constantly use imagery in our lives. Whenever we imagine something, that is a form of imagery. What the mind believes the body can achieve.

Everyone visualizes. In one-third to one-fourth of the population, however, it is so fleeting persons are not conscious of what is going on. It is out of their range of awareness. Imagery is frequently used by psychologists, teachers, athletes, and businesspeople. It hasn't gained acceptance the way meditation is gradually filtering into the mainstream of modern medicine. Imagery means bringing into consciousness things that are already occurring and learning to pay attention to them. It is theorized that conscious expectations about self-healing can relay information to the autonomic nervous system.

The body and mind makes little distinction between the real and imagined. It responds as a unit. Its hard to pin down the exact relationship between behavioral techniques such as imagery and actual physiology and disease outcome. Ironically and paradoxically, psychosomatic symptoms have the greatest success in using imagery to help resolve the illnesses.

The use and influence of imagery in health and disease has significant documentation. But there is still more to understand. Historically, partial understanding has seldom prevented the medical establishment from introducing techniques. Rarely do M.D.'s skillfully apply imagery. There are some reports of terminal illnesses disappearing after the use of this self-healing technique and therapies utilizing the mind. Yet we must remember these dramatic outcomes tend to be the exception rather than the rule.

In my practice I use imagery in a variety of ways. During a meditative session, I use it, as well as recommending patients to incorporate visualizations into their daily lives.

During the 1960's Drs. Carl and Stephanie Simonton developed a program for cancer patients using imagery to promote healing. In their landmark book, *Getting Well Again*, their claims that the immune system could be enhanced by visualizing stronger white blood cells attacking and consuming cancer cells were initially met with considerable criticism and opposition. Of 159 patients involved in their first research project, 19% of the cancers were eliminated completely, 22% were in remission, and those who eventually died doubled their predicted survival time. Data confirming the link integrity of mind and body dates back as far as 1929 when researchers found that thinking about moving a part of the body specifically stimulates nerves in the muscles of that area.

Studies are now being reported in important medical journals that confirm the capacity of the mind to control and direct a wide variety of physiological responses. For example, in a 1983 study at Michigan State University the students learned to control very specific functions of certain white blood cells. It caused an average 60% increase of the neutrophils to leave the blood stream and enter the surrounding tissue. A Harvard University study of relaxation and imagery found an increase of the IGA when using deep breathing and progressive relaxation. They could also increase the T cell function.

We now know that immune responses can be learned. Mice with a fatal autoimmune disorder were trained to prolong their life through a learned response. Jeanne Achterberg, Ph.D., and clinical associate professor in rehabilitation science, says imagery can use all of the senses; some favor one over others. A most potent sense associated with healing is the sense of touch, as we discussed earlier.

Dr. Gerald Epstein, a professor of psychiatry at Mt. Sinai Medical School in New York, has used imagery for several years after a trip to Israel where he met a traditional healer who taught him how to do it. Currently he uses the technique daily in his medical practice, teaches residents and attending physicians how to use it, and has conducted grand rounds on it. He reports dramatic results from spontaneous healings of cancer, as well as significantly reducing healing time of fractures, and notable improvements in a variety of diseases.

Dennis Jaffe, Director of the Family Health Clinic in Los Angeles, helps clients use information acquired during imagery to gather information about their illnesses. These images carry potential meaning, sometimes suggesting significance in the type of illness an individual has. He advises people to dialogue with their images. They often discover they have the capacity to learn and change from their symptoms.

Mental imagery involving emotional topics can stimulate appropriate, even dramatic, body responses. During the 1940's in a study where subjects were instructed to imagine lifting different weights, muscle tension increased with the weight of the imagined lift. Studies show patients with hypertension who used imagery and visualized the blood vessels dilating, lowered their blood pressure much better than those who only used relaxation. Dr. Neal Miller during the 1960's trained rats to increase or decrease their blood pressure on demand by electrically stimulating pleasure centers located in the hypothalamus. The rats eventually became so skilled they could relax or contract specific muscles.

A study at the University of California at San Francisco had asthmatics visualize traveling through the body and improved their breathing. While Australian researchers found good to excellent results in 54% of 121 asthma patients treated with hypnosis, there was a strong correlation between trance depth and positive results. Another researcher discovered that specific cells could be stimulated to decrease tumor growth when visual imagery was used; the process reversed when the practice was stopped.

Combative visualization may not be effective for some cancer patients with unresolved feelings of anger, hate, grief, or loss. When the disease reflects an undischarged emotional energy turned back upon itself, it reinforces such denial.

Repressive patients shouldn't kill but rather love their cancer; to fight a tumor one needs guts, to love a tumor one must draw from deeper resources. Visualization accepts and melts the cancer via a healing gold light emanating from the bone marrow. The emotional content of imagery has been found to have a powerful impact upon the body. Sensual and fear laden images show dramatic physiologic changes. Intense images of negative childhood memories are marked by a jump in the respiratory rate and an increase in the skin's surface tension. Emotions have a great potential for dramatic physical reactions.

Laughter as a Potent, Positive Force

Laughter is one of the most potent healing forces we have access to. During the 1980's health professionals have studied and employed laughter as a therapeutic component in a variety of illnesses. As with other techniques, humor is as old as civilization. In the Bible, Proverbs 17:22 states, "A merry heart doeth good like a medicine, but a broken spirit drieth the bones."

During the late 1970's Norman Cousins popularized laughter as a healing tool for our culture. His book, *Anatomy of an Illness,* chronicled the healing of a frequently terminal rheumatoid condition using laughter and high doses of intravenous vitamin C. Cousins' story has been featured on "Sixty Minutes" and in the country's most prestigious medical journal—*The New England Journal of Medicine.*

During the 1980's studies and conferences on the healing power of laughter were conducted throughout the country. A number of hospitals instituted *laughing rooms* and employed consultants to teach hospital personnel how to use humor and laughter. Patch Adams, M.D., is one of the major proponents of incorporating laughter into the practice of medicine.

Laughter exerts a physiological impact upon the body. It decreases pain, increases the heart rate, consumption of oxygen, and blood pressure. It is also interesting to note that children laugh on the average of 400 times a day—while adults only laugh 15 times daily.

These techniques are just a few examples of the tremendous healing power of the mind. In the future, we can look forward to science continuing to unlock its secrets to assist the process of healing and the maintenance of health.

There is no art of healing in nature, there is only the fact of healing.

—*Deepak Chopra, M.D.*

Chapter 10

Healing the Body

A holistic approach includes assessment of diet—behaviors—lifestyle patterns—consumption of alcohol, nicotine, caffeine and drugs—and physical activity level. At the forefront of preventive health are concerns about diet, lifestyles, and exercise. Over the last ten to fifteen years we've seen a dramatic evolution in the way the public and the medical establishment now views these factors.

Today there is growing interest in nutrition and its long term impact upon the body. On a daily basis the public is provided with new information concerning the vital role diet plays with our health and well-being. Diet and nutrition is at the forefront of our national concern in terms of health. There's also a renaissance of awareness about herbs and vitamins.

The Impact of Diet and Nutrition

The one lecture on nutrition I had in medical school discussed the four basic food groups. It was done in a manner strikingly similar to what I learned in elementary school. Fortunately, the tide has turned and the significance of what we eat is rapidly gaining acceptance.

In general the American diet is high in salt, refined sugar, fat, and calories. These factors increase susceptibility to hypertension, obesity, dental cavities, coronary artery disease, diabetes mellitus, arthritis, gall bladder disease—plus cancer of the breast, colon, rectum, and prostate.

The National Academy of Sciences currently estimates 60% of all cases of cancer in women and 40% of all cases in men are related to nutritional factors. The value of a low fat, high fiber diet in cancer prevention is well documented. There is a clear link between diet and the development of several diseases. Once again this is not to suggest, as with other factors, that diet is the only cause—but it is a significant factor.

There is also growing concern about the safety of our food and water supply in terms of contamination with disease-causing pesticides, pollutants, bacteria, and radiation. Pesticide residues in our food supply have been linked to cancer, neurologic disorders, and birth defects, as well as learning and behavioral disorders in children. Additives, synthetic hormones, and antibiotics also contribute and increase the susceptibility to disease.

Also, the ecological impact of our diet cannot continue to be overlooked. A considerable amount of the forests cleared in North and South America was done for the creation of grazing land for cattle. In the U.S. the vast majority of the grain produced goes to cattle consumption. One acre of land that can produce 20,000 pounds of potatoes, yields only 165 pounds of beef. And it takes five times more grain for meat production, in comparison to human consumption of the grain. Estimates project that if only 10% of the grain used for beef consumption was saved, it could feed the 60 million people who starve to death annually! Each year billions of dollars are spent on electricity and water for meat production.

Science now recognizes that decreasing caloric intake during adulthood can increase longevity. Research has consistently found increased longevity in a variety of animals on restricted diets. The life spans of mice, rats, snails, fish, worms, and monkeys have all been significantly extended with caloric restriction. One study of mice restricted to half of their average food intake showed they lived 55 months—in comparison to the mice on a normal diet living 36 months.

The people of Okinawa lived one hundred years, twice that of the national average, and their incidence of aging-related disease was 30% to 40% lower than the rest of Japan. Yogis in India, with an ultra low caloric intake, reportedly live to be 110 to 120 years old.

During World War II, several European countries were blockaded. In Denmark three million people were forced to become vegetarians. The death rate when food restrictions were the most severe was the lowest in its recorded history. There was a 34% decline from the average number of deaths for the preceding eighteen years. While in Norway doctors found there was a decrease in circulatory disease and death rate; this increased afterwards when food consumption resumed its normal pattern. During the same time, England and Switzerland also experienced significant improvements in health.

After World War II—for the first time on a world wide basis—statistics were complied evaluating diet, incidence of disease, environment, and longevity. It was discovered longevity was not affected by harsh environmental conditions, but was directly related to meat consumption. The groups—including Eskimos, Laplanders, and the Kurgi tribe—who were the highest meat consumers, had the lowest life spans. In comparison, other groups who were living under similarly harsh conditions—but whose diets consisted of less than 5% meat consumption—had the highest life expectancies.

It's most important to strive for variety.

In 1979 the Senate Select Subcommittee on Nutrition made the following recommendations:

1. No single food group contains all the necessary nutrients.

2. Eating different foods will decrease the likelihood of exposure to harmful contaminants that might be found in the food supply.

3. Select foods from each of the following fresh fruits and vegetables:

   • Whole grain breads, cereals, and other products as well as grain such as corn, wheat, rye and rice.

   • Dry peas, beans, legumes, and nuts

   • Animal products, red meat, poultry, fish, and mild cheeses

3. Increase the intake of *un*processed foods; they contain more vitamins and minerals. Processing can remove, reduce, alter, and destroy nutrients—as well as add undesirable contaminants. And processed food is high in salt and sugar.

4. Decrease calories for adults over the age of eighteen.

5. Lower total fat to 40% to 30% of all calories.

6. Reduce saturated fat to no more than one-half of the total fat content.

7. Decrease sugar to less than 10% of total caloric intake.

8. Increase fiber consumption.

The Role of Vitamins and Minerals

Vitamins and minerals are essential to the integrity and function of the body. For many years there has been a controversy about the role vitamin and mineral supplements play in healing and health. The accumulating evidence continually illustrates the role adequate vitamins and mineral intake and therapeutic supplements play in the prevention of disease and the healing process.

Many experts agree that the Recommended Daily Allowance (RDA) requirements are too low and that there is a considerable variability in terms of the physical requirements for vitamins and minerals. These levels were initially established based on studies that identified the lowest amount of each vitamin and mineral that would prevent a clinical vitamin deficiency from occurring. We now know requirements vary from person to person. Variations occur during stress, illness, pregnancy, pollution, and environmental hazards. Also, research is now showing the role that subclinical nutrient deficiencies play in the genesis and treatment of disease.

Melvin R. Werbach, M.D., conducted an extensive review of medical literature. He cited the major nutrient, toxic, and environmental sensitivities that played a role in all of the chronic diseases—including cancer, alcoholism, diabetes, epilepsy, immune disorders, asthma, gall bladder disease, ulcers, fatigue, infertility, infection, hepatitis, multiple sclerosis, kidney stones, arthritis, hypertension, and learning disabilities.

The therapeutic levels are usually megadoses and significantly greater than the RDA requirements. Because these larger dosages can have toxic side effects, it is advisable to take them only under medical supervision. Also, because of the way our food supply is produced, vegetables and fruits are frequently deficient in nutrients. Therefore I routinely recommend nutritional supplementation with a good multivitamin and mineral reparation. Depending on the patient, I make adjustments and frequently add other supplements.

How Herbs Can Contribute to Well-Being

Herbs have also been used for healing since the dawn of history. Today there is a renewed interest in herbs due to a growing concern about the safety of many drugs. Increasing numbers of Americans are turning to herbs, seeking to treat acute and chronic illnesses, and maintain health through herbal supplementation.

Many popular drugs are derived from plants. Penicillin comes from fungus and many chemotherapeutic drugs are also derived from plants, as is digitalis, a potent heart drug.

In the late 1970's, experts testified before the U.S. Senate Subcommittee on Health that an estimated 170,000 American deaths each year are caused by prescribed drugs, especially in older people. The World Health Organization has also recommended the use of herbs as the primary agent of therapy.

Drugs are specific, singular chemical agents that are extremely potent, in terms of suppressing symptoms. They are often toxic with harmful side effects. The difference between a drug and an herb is its potency and the way it effects the body.

The plant contains a variety of compounds that act in concert and are increased by one another. It enhances the body and promotes the natural healing capacity. The numerous compounds in herbs produce overall effects that go beyond the limits of drugs. Herbs tend to function in a capacity that is quite different from a single drug. They regulate and stimulate the organism to promote self-healing. The natural compounds work with the body, in a restorative and healing capacity—in comparison to the isolated single drug or *magic bullet.*

Modern medicine's focus has been to identify one drug that eliminates one symptom. The side effects tend to be much more dangerous and incapacitating than herbs. Botanists and pharmacologists throughout the world are researching literally thousands of plants and are documenting their healing effects. They are beginning to understand the biochemical nature of herbs.

In 1987 the World Health Organization's Dr. Olayiwola Akerele told the meeting of the Society for Economic Botany that industrial countries should not ignore the potential of medicinal plants. "The value of plants in health cannot be disputed," he said.

In the U.S. there is a resurging interest in herbs, while in general they have been more accepted in other parts of the world. For example, in West Germany herbal preparations are sold alongside pharmaceutical drugs. In China, herbal medicine is integrated into the national health-care system, and is used in about 40% of all the cases. Only 15% of the world's population has access to pharmaceutical drugs; it relies on other forms of medication.

Dr. Xavier Lozoya of the Mexican Social Security Institute, a member of the WHO said, "I am absolutely convinced that the future of herbal medicine will be a combination of traditional and modern medicine. The health services will be a new system of integrated systems. We are meant to change the rules of the game.

The Importance of Exercise

The importance of exercise continues to unfold in health and disease prevention. Countless studies document the role of moderate exercise in increasing longevity. It diminishes the risk of developing heart disease by 50%, reduces the toxic physiologic effects of stress and depression, and decreases other chronic diseases including breast and bowel cancer. It also improves the regulation of blood sugar levels in diabetics and lowers lipid (fat) cells.

Also, adults engaged in moderate aerobic exercise for thirty to forty minutes, at least three times a week, realize more benefits than risks. Rigorous exercise does pose somewhat of a risk—including injury and sudden death during exercise.

Exercise improves physiologic adaptation to stress, improves heart and lung fitness, decreases the manifestation of symptoms in the case of mild to moderate arthritis, and increases life expectancy.

A human being is a part of the whole called by us *Universe,* a part limited in time and space. He experiences himself, his thoughts and feelings as something separated from the rest, a kind of optical delusion of his consciousness. This delusion is a kind of prison for us, restricting us to us. Our task must be to free ourselves from this prison by widening our circle of compassion to embrace all living creatures and the whole nature in its beauty.

—*Albert Einstein*

Chapter 11

Healing Ourselves, Healing Our World

We live in a world marked by escalating confusion, chaos, and conflict. Our earth's ecological system in the last one hundred years has been severely damaged by the wanton abuse of industrialization, with little relief in sight. The crisis of the individual parallels those of the family, community, and nation. And the threat of thermonuclear warfare and total destruction can never be ignored.

Several years ago I was at a conference on world peace. There was a controversial discussion about the likelihood of nuclear war. Most of the participants felt there was a good chance the superpowers would one day start a conflict that could lead to the destruction of the planet. I was in agreement with the majority of the group, until I heard a man speak about his experiences after World War II. He decided he wanted to visit Hiroshima and Nagasaki, to see the destruction for himself. He said it was one thing to see the pictures, and another to actually experience it.

When he saw the shadows of children who were burned onto the walls, at that moment he made a commitment to devote his life to the cause of world peace. He pledged the rest of his life to this cause so, "No other child on this planet would ever have to suffer such a horrible death." I don't recall this man's first name, but his words and face are ingrained in my memory. For the first time in my life, I felt that the carnage, death, and destruction could be avoided. I was riveted into a place of hope I'd never known before. At that moment in my heart I knew another way was possible, and that peace could in fact become the foundation of our realty.

Becoming Brothers and Sisters

I heard someone articulate what has always been in my heart, "World War III is not inevitable. But to avoid it, we must heal and resolve that which involves us...that which prevents us from seeking each other as brothers and sisters." In many ways, this is a time of great turmoil and upheaval on the earth. Trillions of dollars are spent each year for weapons by the vast majority of the governments in the world. Yet in 1989 UNICEF estimates that during the 1990's over 100,000,000 will die. Each day over 40,000 children die and half of these deaths could be prevented or treated. The report also estimates that if one day's worth of military spending was devoted to children's health, most of the diseases could be wiped out.

Perhaps this is the time to provide an opportunity to heal the barriers that cause our distorted views of the world. Hopefully the healing of individuals will lead to healing relationships, communities, nations, and our entire global village.

The potential for healing, health, and transformation rests not only in the individual, but within every element and aspect of our world that is diseased and out of harmony with the whole. As a physician, I cannot merely focus on sending those who have been healed of their emotional and physical maladies back into a diseased environment. I must be concerned about the environmental, political, social, cultural, and economic realities that shape our world.

Getting Aligned with Love and Harmony

As a friend of mine appropriately said, "In this life, if you are not in alignment with love, then you are out of harmony with life. If you fail to see the unity and interrelatedness of all things, then you are missing the boat."

This book was written from a desire to share many of the experiences that have blessed my life and enriched my days. It is my hope that if it does promote healing, then the transformations will contribute to the whole—to the healing of our world, ourselves, our children, and the generations yet to come.

There is an ancient Egyptian proverb that says, "Each child comes with the message that God is not yet discouraged of man." May we all keep faith, hope, and love alive in our hearts, in order that we might heal ourselves...and our world.

Go in peace. And until we meet again, may the light of love, healing, and joy smile upon your spirit.

Appendices

As discussed throughout this book, a holistic approach encompasses all aspects of being—including body, mind, and spirit. Because the body heals itself, each healing technique I use has its place. It is not the focus of therapy, eliciting the inner healing response is. It is frequently difficult to determine which technique actually stimulated the healing process; the synergistic effects of several therapies often do what one or two alone cannot.

These appendices include a sampling of several holistic healing techniques that I have used in my practice. By no means is it all-inclusive, nor is it recommended these therapies be used instead of seeking the assistance of a physician. This section is included only for informational purposes.

Attitude: Assuming Responsibility for Your State of Health

In terms of a holistic approach to health, it is very important for the individual to assume responsibility for her or his health and healing. This is a very different perspective from accepting blame and guilt. Even though there are many factors beyond our control, it is important to understand we play a significant role in our health and healing—as well as the development of disease.

I encourage my patients to find a happy medium between the *you create your own reality* mind-set and the *disease just falls from the sky* belief. Taking responsibility in a balanced way, promotes and recognizes how the choices we make in terms of lifestyle, dietary, work, and behavioral and emotional patterns affect our susceptibility to disease and facilitation of health.

Often I suggest my patients keep a journal of activities, diet, work habits, thoughts, and feelings for a month in order to increase their understanding of their behavior. This process of writing is often quite helpful to them.

There are several recommendations that I make.

These keys to health commonly include:

1. Exercise regularly, at least three times a week for thirty minutes.

2. Eat healthy foods—focus on increasing your consumption of fresh fruits, vegetables, and grains; diminish intake of processed foods, sugar, salt, and foods with dyes, preservatives, and additives. Significantly reduce or abandon your consumption of alcohol, nicotine, and caffeine.

3. Get adequate sleep.

4. Relax regularly through whatever means you find enjoyable, including participating in a hobby or another desirable activity away from *work*.

5. Resolve anger and fear daily.

6. Develop meaningful relationships with friends and family.

7. Maintain weight within 10% of your ideal body weight.

8. Spend quiet time with yourself each day, at least ten minutes focusing on the day and your feelings.

9. Be honest with yourself. The old saying *To thine own self be true* is very important to your health and healing.

10. Be gentle with yourself. Treat yourself and others with kindness and consideration.

11. Be forgiving of yourself and others on a daily basis.

12. Learn to listen to your feelings and to others.

13. Find ways to accommodate the needs of your spirit.

Life Review: A Series of Penetrating Questions

To facilitate understanding and awareness of one's emotional needs and other aspects of being, I frequently give my patients a quiz—one they can't fail. I call it the *Life Survey* because there are a series of questions about their lives. There are no right or wrong answers, only honest or dishonest ones. Why don't you give it a try?

1. In general are you happy and contented with your life?

2. If so why, if not, why not?

3. What if anything would you change in your life at this time?

4. Are you happy with your chosen vocation?

5. Are you happy with your friendships?

6. Are you happy with your relationship with your family?

7. Are you happy with your romantic relationship?

8. Are you happy with yourself?

9. What's more important to you, your opinion of yourself or what others think of you?

10. How would you characterize each of the following: your relationships with your family, parents, children, friends, significant other, coworkers and neighbors?

11. Describe the most significant memories you have of your childhood.

12. Describe your *best* and *worst* qualities.

13. You found out you had only one day, one week, one month, or one year to live. What would you do in each case?

14. What is your greatest regret in life?

15. What is your greatest joy in life?

16. What are your goals in life at this time; what were they when you were an adolescent and young adult?

17. What area of your life would you like to change the most?

18. What are the important dreams in this life that you have yet to achieve?

19. What is the most difficult and challenging part of your life?

20. What is the most joyous and fulfilling part of your life?

Meditation and Visualization:
An Introduction

There are many ways to meditate and visualize. In my practice I utilize the simplest techniques. These exercises can facilitate the healing process. All of the meditations and visualizations are modifications of Exercise #1, so follow the basic steps with each one.

Exercise 1 — Basic Meditation:

Find a quiet place in your home or office where you can meditate for several minutes without any disruption. Unplug the phone, turn off the radio or television, and close the door if there are others in the house so you can create a space conducive to meditating. For beginners, it may be difficult to remember the instructions, so I recommend having someone read the steps to you or to make a tape and play it back.

Sit or lie down. Whatever position you assume allow the spine to be as straight as possible. Many mediators find the lotus position, sitting with the legs crossed, is most conducive; others, myself included, prefer lying down. Soft, quiet music can assist the process.

Begin by focusing on your breathing. Take a few deep breaths, breathing in through the nose and out through the mouth, very slowly. The expiration should be approximately twice the length of the intake.

Become aware of your body. Notice its presence and allow your mind to scan your whole physical being, noting how it is resting, how it feels, if there's any pain, tension, or discomfort present.

Gradually begin to relax your body beginning at the top of your head. Very slowly move down your body, relaxing your scalp, forehead, eyes, ears, sinuses, muscles, nose, tongue, lips, teeth, neck, esophagus, larynx, thyroid gland, and lymph nodes in the neck. Now relax your ribs, spine, chest, all of the muscles in your chest, your lungs, heart, nerves, diaphragm, abdomen, stomach, liver, spleen, gall bladder, intestines, colon, pelvic bone, thighs, muscles, knees, legs, and feet.

Relax your entire body, going deeper and deeper and deeper. Your body feels heavier as you go deeper into this state. You may feel any irregularities, tension, pain, or discomfort being released from your body. Let it go into the universe with love as a wave of relaxation flows over it. Allow yourself to feel the peace your body is experiencing. Become completely aware of this state of peace.

After a few minutes, when you are ready, gradually begin to return to your normal state of awareness. Take a few minutes to return your breathing to its normal pattern.

Exercise 2 – Focusing Meditation:

Follow the same steps as you took in Exercise 1. Once you are in a state of deep relaxation, focus on one thought: love, peace, healing, health, compassion, harmony, etc.

Exercise 3 – Light Meditation:

Once you have entered a meditative state, begin to visualize light. Imagine a beautiful glowing ball of white light is located about six to twelve inches over your head. It's not necessary for you to see it. You can feel it, hear it, or experience the light in whatever way is appropriate for you. There is no right or wrong way to meditate. Just do what feels best.

Allow the light to enter through the top of your head and slowly fill and surround your body. If there are areas difficult for the light to flow through, concentrate on them. Let the irregularities, blocks, and imbalances to be released from your body. Slowly allow the light to intensify as much as possible without causing your body discomfort.

As the light flows through your entire body, see it exiting through the bottom of your feet. Once again when you feel the process is completed, slowly release the light and gradually return to your normal state of awareness.

Exercise 4 – Rainbow Meditation:

This is similar to Exercise 3, except after the white light has become as intensified as possible, begin to change the colors. Start with a deep dark maroon, red, orange, gold, pink, green, blue, and violet. Once you've visualized all of the colors, allow a rainbow to fill your body.

When you've completed it, once again release the light and slowly return to your normal state.

Exercise 5 – Chakra Meditation:

Using the techniques of Exercise 1, instead of allowing the light to enter your entire body, see a column of light flowing along the spine. As it reaches the base of the spine, see a cone-shaped wheel of light with the tip beginning at the base of the spine. Visualize the chakra spinning in a clockwise fashion from the outside of your body, or counterclockwise from the inside. Allow the light to become as intense as possible. Once again, if you have difficulty seeing the light, feel it–sense it–or hear its presence. After a few minutes, allowing this light to continue at the first center, see another sphere at the second center located at the center of your pelvic area (A diagram of the chakras here appears on page 219.) Do the same at this center, and continue this process at the center of the abdomen, the center of the chest, at the heart, the middle of your throat, forehead, and at the top of your head.

Once again complete the process, release the light, and slowly return to your normal state of consciousness and breathing.

The same meditation can be performed using different colors at each chakra, beginning with dark maroon at the first, orange at the second, yellow at the third, green at the fourth, blue at the fifth, violet at the sixth, and white at the seventh.

Exercise 6 – Healing the Emotions:

Once you are in a meditative state, begin to focus on your fourth chakra, your heart center. Allow any painful feelings and experiences to come to the surface. When an old pain and experience does surface, surround the pain with a beautiful glowing white light. Intensify the light as much as possible. When the light has reached its greatest intensity, begin to release the memory and the pain into the universe of love.

When the process is completed, gradually return to your normal state.

Exercise 7 – Forgiveness:

Once you've entered a meditative state, focus on a part of yourself you would like to forgive. When you have a good image of what it is, see yourself sitting in a chair facing this aspect of your being. Very slowly, begin to send this aspect of light from your heart. Surround it, and your entire being, with light. Allow the light to bathe the entire picture. With the light, consciously send unconditional love and complete acceptance to the portion of you that needs to be forgiven. As you send this love, allow the aspect to slowly dissolve in your presence. Complete the process, releasing the light and returning to your normal state. This exercise can also be used to forgive others.

Affirmations: Powerful Healing Tools

Affirmations are among the most powerful healing tools known to exist. They can be used anytime and anywhere to facilitate the healing process. Here are a few I frequently use in my practice.

1. I am a child of the universe and I am loved.

2. Today, I am healing, whole, and complete.

3. My body is capable of complete health and an encompassing healing.

4. I am healing the disease that is currently residing in my body.

5. Each day I am becoming stronger, healthier, and more complete.

6. Healing and health are my inalienable birthright.

7. I am committing myself to living each day as it comes. I cannot change yesterday and can best affect tomorrow by living fully today.

8. Each moment I am honestly attempting to acknowledge my thoughts, feelings, joy, and pain.

9. I am not guilty of causing disease, but am responsible for my health and healing.

The Chakras: A Diagram

*7th Crown is located at the top of the head and is associated with the functioning of the entire nervous system (central and peripheral). It is through this center that the energies enter to nourish the other chakras as well. The seventh chakra is associated with spiritual questing.

*6th Pituitary is found at the center of the forehead. This *third eye* center is associated with our intuition. It is intimately involved with the functioning of the pituitary and pineal glands, although some systems assign the pineal to the crown center. The physical structures governed by this chakra include the eyes, ears, nose, and sinuses.

*5th Throat is the communication chakra located at the middle of the neck, over the area where the thyroid gland and larynx are located. This center is associated with the thyroid, parathyroid gland and the cervical ganglia, trachea, esophagus, and cervical vertebrae. As the communication center, it governs any form of expression, including creativity.

*4th Heart is that within the physical body that helps to regulate the function of the heart and the internal thoracic organs, including the thymus gland, heart plexus, ribs, lungs, major lymph glands, and the diaphragm. It is most commonly located at the very center of the chest, between the breasts, over the sternum. In a few individuals it is deviated to the left and resides directly over the physical heart. This center is associated with the giving and receiving of love in all of its forms in our relationships. The heart

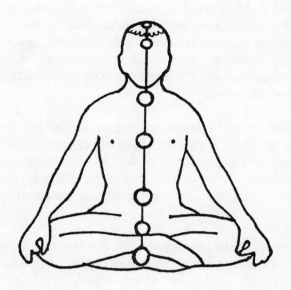

chakra is intimately involved with any form of healing and is believed to be the anchor of the soul.

*3rd Solar plexus is associated with the pancreas and the solar nerve plexus. It influences the abdominal organs of digestion—liver, gall bladder, intestines, spleen, stomach, and lumbar vertebrae. On the psychospiritual level it is related to our self-identity in relation to others.

*2nd Sexual chakra is located in the pelvic area and is involved with the organs of reproduction (ovaries and testes), bladder, colon (large intestines), and the sacrum. This center primarily focuses on the expression of our feminine or masculine identity and sexuality.

*1st Root chakra is found at the base of the spine and is different from the other centers because it is primarily the endocrine gland. The adrenals are not located in adjacent proximity to the center. It is also associated with the coccyx and orifices of excretion. The root center is responsible for our *groundedness* in terms of one's daily relationship with the external world and link to the earth.

The recognition of these nonphysical forms—as well as the use of other therapies including the laying on of hands and homeopathy—are on the forefront of the evolving, holistic healing arts. They possess a vast potential and promise for all involved with and seeking healing and health.

Bibliography

Books

Archterberg J. *Imagery in Healing: Shamanism and Modern Medicine*. 1985, San Francisco: Shambhala.

Ader R. *Psychoneuroimmunology*. 1981, New York: Academic Press.

Afrika L. *African Holistic Health*. 1989, Silver Spring, MD: Adesegun, Johnson and Koram Publishers.

Alexander F. *Psychosomatic Medicine*. 1950, New York: W.W. Norton.

Aron E. and Aron A. *The Maharishi Effect-Scientific Discovery of the Astounding Power of Group Mind*. 1986, Walpoint, NH: Stillpoint Publishing.

Appiah-Kubi J. *Man Cures, God Heals*. 1981, New York: Friendship Press.

Arehart-Truchel, J. *Biotypes: The Critical Link Between Your Personality and Your Health*. 1980, New York: Times Books, Quandrangle/The New York Times Book Co., Inc.

Bauman E, et al. *The Holistic Health Lifebook: A Guide to Personal and Planetary Well-Being*. 1981, Berkeley, CA: And/Or Press Inc.

Bauman E. *The New Holistic Health Handbook: Living Well in a New Age*. 1985, Lexington, MA: The Stephen Greene Press.

Becher R. and Marino A. *Electromagnetism and Life*. 1982, Albany, New York: State University Press of New York.

Bendit J. and Bendit P. *The Etheric Body of Man: The Bridge of Consciousness*. 1969, Wheaton, IL: Theosophical Publishing House.

Benson H. and Klipper M. *The Relaxation Response*. 1975, New York: Avon Books.

Benson H. *Beyond the Relaxation Response*. 1984, New York: Berkeley Books.

Benson H. *Your Maximum Mind*. 1988, New York: Times Books.

Borysenko J. *Minding the Body, Minding the Mind*. 1987, Boston: Addison-Wesley Publishing Co.

Briggs J. and Plat F. *Looking Glass Universe: The Emerging Science of Wholeness*. 1984, New York: Simon and Schuster.

Brody H. *Placebos and the Philosophy of Medicine*. 1977, Chicago: University of Chicago Press.

Burr, H. *The Fields Of Life: Our Links With the Universe*. 1972, New York: Ballantine Books.

Carlson R. and Benjamin S. *Healers on Healing*. 1989, Los Angeles: Jeremy P. Tarcher, Inc.

Capra F. *The Tao Of Physics*. 1977, New York: Bantam Books.

Capra F. *The Turning Point: Science, Society and the Rising Culture*. 1982, New York: Simon and Schuster.

Carper J. *The Food Pharmacy*. 1988, New York: Bantam Books.

Ceruiti E. *Mystic with the Healing Hands: The Life Story of Olga Worral*. 1977, New York: Harper and Row.

Chopra D. *Quantum Healing*. 1989, New York: Bantam Books.

Church D. and Sherr A. *The Heart of the Healer*. 1987, New York: Penguin Books.

Cousens G. *Spiritual Nutrition and the Rainbow Diet*. 1986, Boulder, CO: Cassandra Press.

Cousins N. *Anatomy of An Illness*. 1981, New York: Bantam Books.

Cousins N. *The Healing Heart*. 1983, New York: W.W. Norton.

Cranton E. and Brecher A. *Bypassing Bypass: The New Techniques of Chelation Therapy*. 1984, New York: Stein and Day Publishers.

Crile G. *Surgery: Your Choices, Your Alternatives*. 1978, New York: Dell Publishing Company.

Davis A. *Let's Stay Healthy*. 1981, New York: Harcourt, Brace, Jovanovich, Inc.

Dumietrescu I. and Kenyon J. *Electrographic Imaging in Medicine and Biology*. 1983, Suffolk, Great Britain: Neville Spearman Ltd.

Epstein G. *Healing Visualizations: Creating Health Through Imagery*. 1989, New York: Bantam Books.

Ferguson T. (ed.) *Medical Self-Care*. 1980, New York, Summit Books.

Frank J. *Persuasion and Healing*. 1974, New York: Schocken Books.

Fromm E. *The Revolution of Hope: Toward a Humanized Technology*. 1968, New York: Harper and Row.

Fuilder S. *The Tao of Medicine*. 1980, Rochester VT: Destiny Books.

Galvani L. *Commentary on the Effects of Electricity*. (trans) M Foley. 1953, Norwalk, CT: Burndy Library.

Garrat A. *Electrophysiology and Electrotherapeutics*. 1969, Boston: Ticknos and Fields.

Gerber R. *Vibrational Medicine: New Choices for Healing Ourselves*. 1988, Santa Fe, NM: Bear and Co.

Gres H. and Dick W. *The New Soviet Psychic Discoveries*. 1978, New York: Warner Books.

Hammond S. *We Are All Healers*. 1973, New York: Ballantine Books.

Harrison J. *Love Your Disease*. 1988, Santa Monica, CA: Hay House, Inc.

Horowitz L. *Taking Charge*. 1988, New York: Random House.

Jaffe D. *Healing From Within*. 1980, New York: Alfred A. Knopf.

Jampolsky G. *Love is Letting Go of Fear*. 1979, Mullbrae, CA: Celestial Arts.

Jonas S. *Health Care Delivery in the United States*. 1981, New York: Spinger Publishing Co., Inc.

Joy W.B. *Joy's Way*. 1979, Los Angeles: Jeremy P. Tarcher, Inc.

Justice B. *Who Gets Sick*. 1987, Los Angeles, Jeremy P. Tarcher, Inc.

Kadans J. *Encyclopedia of Medicinal Herbs*. 1970, New York: Arco Publishing Co.

Kakar S. *Shamans, Mystics and Doctors*. 1982, New York: Alfred A. Knopf.

Kenyon J. *Modern Techniques of Acupuncture: Vol 3*. 1985, Wellingborough, Northampshire, Great Britain: Thorson's Publishers Ltd.

Kilner W. *The Human Aura*. 1965, Secaucus, NJ: The Citadel Press.

Krieger D. *Therapeutic Touch: How to Use Your Hands to Help or to Heal*. 1979, Englewood Cliffs, NJ: Prentice Hall, Inc.

Krieger D. *Foundations of Holistic Health Nursing: The Renaissance Nurse*. 1981, New York: Lippincott.

Krippner S. and Albo V. *The Realms of Healing*. 1976, Mellbrae, CA: Celestial Arts.

Krippner S. and Albo V. *The Healing States*. 1987, New York: Fireside Books.

Kunz D. (ed.) *Spiritual Aspects of the Healing Arts*. 1985, Wheaton, IL: Theosophical Publishing Company

Lalone M. *A New Perspective on the Health of Canadians*. 1974, Ottawa, Canada: Government of Canada.

Larson B. *There's a Lot More to Health Than Not Being Sick*. 1984, Waco, TX: Word Books.

Litman T. and Robins L. *Health Politics and Policy*. 1984, New York: John Wiley and Sons.

Locke S. and Douglas C. *The Healer Within: The New Medicine of Mind and Body*. 1986, New York: E.P. Dutton.

McGarey W. *Acupuncture and Body Energies*. 1974, Phoenix, AZ: Gabriel Press.

McMahon C. *Where Medicine Fails*. 1986, New York: Conch Magazine Limited.

Meek G. *Healers and the Healing Process*. 1977, Wheaton, IL: Theospohical Publishing House.

Mendelsohn R. *Confessions of a Medical Heretic*. 1979, New York: Warner Books.

Moss, T. *The Body Electric*. 1979, Los Angeles: Jeremy P. Tarcher, Inc.

Motoyama H. *The Functional Relationship Between Yoga Asanas and Acupuncture Meridians*. 1979, Tokyo, Japan: IARP.

Motoyama H. *Theories of the Chakras: Bridge to Higher Consciousness*. 1981, Wheaton, IL: Theosophical Publishing House.

Needleman J. *A Sense of the Cosmos: The Encounter of Modern Science and Ancient Truth*. 1977, New York: E.P. Dutton.

Nieper H. *Revolution in Technology and Society*. 1985, Oldenberg, Federal Republic of Germany: MIT Verlag.

Ornstein R. *The Psychology of Consciousness*. 1972, San Francisco: W.H. Freeman.

Ostrander S. and Schroeder L. *Psychic Discoveries Behind the Iron Curtain*. 1970, Englewood Cliffs, NJ: Prentice Hall.

Pearsall P. *Superimmunity*. 1985, New York: Fawcett Gold Medal.

Peck M. *The Road Less Travelled: A New Psychology of Love and Spiritual Growth*. 1978, New York: Touchstone Books.

Peele N. *The Power of Positive Thinking*. 1955, Englewood Cliffs, NJ: Prentice Hall.

Pelletier K. *Mind as Healer, Mind as Slayer*. 1977, New York: Dell Publishing Company.

Pelletier K. *Holistic Medicine*. 1979, New York: Delacorte Press/Seymour Lawrance.

Pierrakas J. *The Human Energy Systems Theory*. 1975, New York: Institute for the New Age.

Popenoe C. *Wellness*. 1977, Washington, DC: Yes! Inc.

Potter J. *How to Improve Your Odds Against Cancer*. 1988, Hollywood, FL: Frederick Fell Publishers.

Powell A. *The Etheric Double: The Health Aura of Man*. 1969, Wheaton, IL: Theosophical Publishing House.

Price V. *Type A Behavior Pattern: A Model for Research and Practice*. 1982, New York: Academic Press.

Rama S. *A Practical Guide to Holistic Health*. 1983, Honesdale, PA: The Himalayan International Institute.

Ray B. *The Reiki Factor*. 1983, St Petersburg, FL: Radiance Associates.

Reich W. *The Discovery of the Orgone, Vol 1: The Function of the Organism* (trans) T Waye. 1942, New York: Farrar, Straus and Giroux.

Reich W. *The Discovery of Orgone, Vol 2: The Cancer Biopathy* (trans) T. Waye. 1978, New York: Orgone Institute.

Rose J. *The Herbal Body Book*. 1976, New York: Gross and Dunlap.

Rosenburg H. *The Doctor's Book of Vitamin Therapy*. 1979, New York: G.P. Putnam's Sons.

Rosenfield I. *Modern Prevention*. 1987, New York, Bantam Books.

Rossman M. *Healing Yourself*. 1987, New York: Pocket Books.

Russel P. *The Global Brain*. 1986, Los Angeles: Jeremy P. Tarcher, Inc.

Ryan R. and Travis J. *The Wellness Workbook*. 1981, Berkeley, CA: Ten Speed Press.

Samuels M. and Samuels N. *The Well Adult*. 1980, New York: Summit Books.

Selye H. *Stress Without Distress*. 1974, New York: New American Library.

Selye H. *The Stress Of Life*. 1976, New York: McGraw-Hill.

Siegel B. *Love, Medicine and Miracles*. 1986, New York: Harper and Row.

Siegel B. *Peace, Love and Healing*. 1989, New York: Harper and Row.

Simonton O., Simonton S. and Creighton J. *Getting Well Again*. 1981, New York: Bantam Books.

Smuts J. *Holism and Evolution*. 1926, New York: Viking Press.

Sontag S. *Illness as Metaphor*. 1978, New York: Vintage Press.

Starr P. *The Social Transformation of American Medicine*. 1973, New York: Basic Books.

Talbot M. *Mysticism and the New Physics*. 1980, New York: Bantam Books.

Tierra M. *Planetary Herbology*. 1988, Santa Fe, NM: Lotus Press.

Weil A. *Health and Healing*. 1983, Boston: Houghton, Mifflin Co.

Wensel L. *Acupuncture for Americans*. 1980, Reston, VA: Reston Publishing Co., Inc.

Werbach M. *Nutritional Influences on Illness: A Sourcebook of Clinical Research*. 1988, Tarzana, CA: Third Line Press.

White J. *Frontiers of Consciousness*. 1974, New York: Avon Books.

White J. and Krippner S. (eds.) *Future Science: Life Energies and the Physics of Paranormal Phenomena*. 1977, New York: Doubleday.

Wohl S. *The Medical Industrial Complex*. 1984, New York: Crown Publishers.

Worral A. and Worral O. *The Gift of Healing*. 1977, Columbus, OH: Ariel Press.

Zukav G. *The Dancing Wu Li Masters: An Overview of the New Physics*. 1979, New York: William Morrow and Company.

Review Articles

Adler H. "The Doctor-Patient Relationship Revisited: An Analysis of the Placebo Effect." Annals of Internal Medicine 78 (1973) pp. 595-598.

Allison J. "Respiration Changes During Transcendental Meditation." Lancet i (1970) pp. 833-834.

Anand B., Chima G. and Singh B. "Some Aspects of Electroencephalographic Studies in Yogis." Electroencephalography and Clinical Neurophysiology 13 (1961) pp. 452-456.

Barefoot J. "Hostility, Coronary Heart Disease Incidence, and Total Mortality: A Twenty-five Year Follow-up Study of 255 Physicians." Psychosomatic Medicine 45 (1983) pp. 59-63.

Bajusz E. and Selye H. "The Chemical Prevention of Cardiac Neuroses Following Occlusion of Coronary Vessels." Canadian Medical Journal 82 (1960) p. 212.

Beecher H. "The Powerful Placebo." Journal of the American Medical Association 159 (1955) pp. 1602-1606.

Becher M. "Three Cardiologists Report Prayers for Their Patients Are *Answered*." Medical Tribune (January 8, 1986) pp. 3, 15.

Benson H. and Wallace R. "Decreased Drug Abuse with Transcendental Meditation-A Study of 1,862 Subjects." 1972, In Drug Abuse-Proceedings of International Conference, edited C.J. Zarafonetis, Philadelphia: Lea and Febiger, pp. 369-376.

Benson H., Rosner B., Marzetta B. and Klemchick H. "Decreased Blood Pressure in Pharmacologically Treated Hypertensive Patients Who Regularly Elicited the Relaxation Response." Lancit i (1974) pp. 289-291.

Benson H. "The Placebo Effect: A Neglected Asset in the Care of Patients." Journal of the American Medical Association 232 (1975) pp. 1225-1227.

Benson H. "Systemic Hypertension and the Relaxation Response." New England Journal of Medicine 296 (1977) pp. 1152-1156.

Benson H. "Temperature Changes During the Practice of g Tum-mo Yoga." Nature 298 (1982) p. 402

Benson H. "The Relaxation Response: History, Physiologic Bases and Clinical Usefulness." Acta Medica Scandinavica (Supplementum) 660 (1982) pp. 231-237.

Blumberg E., West P. and Ellis F. "A Possible Relationship Between Psychological Factors and Human Cancer." Psychosomatic Medicine 16 (1954) pp. 277-286.

Borysenko J. "Healing Motives: An Interview with David C. McClelland." Advances 2 (1985) pp. 29-41.

Braverman E. and Pfeiffer C. "Essential Trace Elements and Cancer." Journal of Orthomolecular Psychiatry 11 (1982) pp. 28-41.

Brennan B. "Function of the Human Energy Field in the Dynamic Process of Health, Healing and Disease." Monograph, 1980, New York: Institute for the New Age.

Burr H. and Lane C. "Electrical Characteristics of Living Systems." Yale Journal of Biology and Medicine 8 (1935) pp. 31-35.

Burr H. and Northrop F. "The Electro-Dynamic Theory of Life." Quality Review of Biology 10 (1935) pp. 322-333.

Burr H. "The Meaning of Bio-Electric Potentials." Yale Journal of Biology and Medicine 16 (1944) pp. 353-360.

Capra F. "The New Vision of Reality. Toward a Synthesis of Eastern Wisdom and Western Science," in Ancient Wisdom and Modern Science, ed. S. Grof, 1984, Albany, NY: State University of New York Press.

Carrington P. "The use of Meditation-Relaxation Techniques for the Management of Stress in a Working Population." Journal of Occupational Medicine 22 (1980) pp. 221-231.

Cassell J. "The Relation of the Urban Environment to Health: Implications for Prevention." Mt. Sinai Journal of Medicine 40 (1973) pp. 539-550.

Cooper M. "A Relaxation Technique in the Management of Hypercholesterolemia." Journal of Human Stress 1 (1979) pp. 24-27.

Cousins N. "Anatomy of an Illness: As Perceived by a Patient." New England Journal of Medicine 295 (1976) pp. 1458-1463.

Cranton E. "Current Status of EDTA Chelation Therapy in Occlusive Arterial Disease." Journal of Holistic Medicine 4 (1982) pp. 24-33/

Evans F. "The Placebo Response in Pain Control." Psychopharmacology Bulletin 17 (1974) pp. 72-79.

Finch C. "The African Background of Medical Science." (ed) I Van Sertima, *Blacks in Science*. 1983, New Brunswick, NJ: Journal of African Civilizations Ltd., pp. 148-155.

Finch C. "Science and Symbol in Egyptian Medicine: Commentaries on the Edwin Smith Papyrus." (ed) I Van Sertima, Egypt Revisited. 1990, New Brunswick, NJ: Journal of African Civilizations Ltd.

Frank J. "The Faith That Heals." Johns Hopkins Medical Journal 137 (1975) pp. 127-131.

Goodwin J. "Knowledge and Use of Placebos by House Officers and Nurses." Annals of Internal Medicine 91 (1979) pp. 106-110.

Grad B., Cadoret R. and Paul G. "The Influence of an Unorthodox Method of Treatment of Wound Healing in Mice." International Journal of Parapsychology 3 (1961) pp. 5-24.

Grad B. "A Telekinetic Effect on Plant Growth." International Journal of Parapsychology 5 (1963) pp. 117-133.

Grad B. "A Telekinetic Effect on Plant Growth II. Experiments Involving Treatment of Saline in Stoppered Bottles." International Journal of Parapsychology 6 (1964) pp. 473-498.

Grad B. "Some Biological Effects of the Laying-On-Of-Hands: A Review of Experiments with Animals and Plants." Journal of the American Society for Psychical Research 59 (1965) pp. 95-127.

Grad B. "The Laying-On-Of-Hands: Implications for Psychotherapy, Gentling and the Placebo Effect." Journal of the American Society for Psychical Research 61 (1967) pp. 286-305.

Grad B. "Healing by the Laying-On-Of-Hands: Review of Experiments and Implications." Pastoral Psychology 21 (1970) pp. 19-26.

Grad B. "Healing by the Laying-On-Of-Hands: A Review of Experiments." (ed) D Sobel. *Ways of Health: Holistic Approaches to Ancient and Contemporary Medicine*. 1979, New York: Harcourt, Brace, Jovanovich.

Grier S. "Psychological Response to Breast Cancer. Effect on Outcome." Lancet 13 (1979) pp. 785-787.

Hunt V., Massey W., Weinberg R., Bruvere R. and Hahn P. Project Report. "A Study of Structural Integration from Neuromuscular, Energy Field and Emotional Approaches." 1977, Los Angeles: UCLA.

Kaplan N. "Therapy for Mild Hypertension: Toward a More Balanced View." Journal of the American Medical Association 249 (1983) pp. 365-367.

Killer E. and Bzdek V. "Effects of Therapeutic Touch on Tension Headache Pain." Nursing Research 35 (1986) pp. 101-105.

Kirlian S. and Kirlian V. "Photography and Visual Observations by Means of High Frequency Currents." Journal of Scientific and Applied Photography: 6 pp. 145-148.

Kirlian Photography Fighting For Toehold in U.S. Medicine. Medical News. March 6, 1978, p. 24.

Karagulla S. "Energy Fields and Medical Diagnosis. (ed) Regush N. *The Human Aura*. 1974, New York: Berkeley Publishing.

Krieger D. "The Response of In-Vivo Human Hemoglobin to an Active Healing Therapy by Direct Laying on of Hands." Human Dimensions 1 (1972) pp. 12-15.

Krieger D. "The Relationship of Touch with the Intent to Help or Heal, to Subjects' In Vivo Hemoglobin Values: A Study in Personalized Interaction." In Proceedings of the Ninth American Nurses' Association Research Conference. 1973, New York: American Nurses' Association. pp. 39-58.

Krieger D. "Healing by the Laying-On of Hands as a Facilitator of Bioenergetic Change: The Response of In-Vivo Human Hemoglobin. Psychoenergetic Systems 1 (1974) pp. 121-129.

Krieger D. "Therapeutic Touch: The Imprimatur of Nursing." American Journal of Nursing 5 (1975) pp. 748-787.

Krieger D., Peper E., and Ancoli S. "Physiologic Indicies of Therapeutic Touch." American Journal of Nursing 4 (1974) pp. 660-662.

Langone J. "Acupuncture: New Respect for an Ancient Remedy." Discover, August 9, 1984, pp. 70-73.

Lehman L. "Nonpharmacologic Therapy of Blood Pressure." General Hospital Psychiatry 4 (1982) pp. 27-32.

LeShan L. "Psychological States as Factors in the Development of Malignant Disease: A Critical Review." Journal of the National Cancer Institute 22 (1959) pp. 1-18.

Levine A. "American Business is Bullish on Wellness." Medical World News, March 29, 1982 p. 32.

Locke S. "Stress, Adaptation, and Immunity." General Hospital Psychiatry 4 (1982) pp. 49-58.

Lowinger P. "What Makes the Placebo Work?" Archives of General Psychiatry 20 (1969) pp. 80-88.

Mack R. "Occasional Notes. Lessons from Living with Cancer." New England Journal of Medicine 311 (1984) pp. 1642-1643.

Mall S. Kirlian Photography in Cancer Diagnosis. Osteopathic Physician 1978. 45(5), pp. 24-27.

Martin R. "Sense of Humor as a Moderator of the Relation Between Stressors and Moods." Journal of Personality and Social Psychology 45 (1983) pp. 1313-1324.

Mason R. "Acceptance and Healing." Journal of Religion and Health 8 (1969) pp. 123-142.

Miller J. "Immunity and Crises, Large and Small." Science News, May 31, 1986, p. 340.

Patel C. "Yoga and Biofeedback in the Management of Hypertension." Lancet ii (1973) pp. 1053-1055.

Patel C. "Twelve Month Follow-up of Yoga and Biofeedback in the Management of Hypertension." Lancet (1975) pp. 62-64.

Pepper O. "A Note on the Placebo." American Journal of Pharmacy 117 (1945) pp. 409-412.

Quinn J. "Therapeutic Touch as Energy Exchange: Testing the Theory." Advances in Nursing Science 6 (1984) pp. 47-49.

Rabkin J. and Streuning E. "Life Events, Stress and Illness." Science 194 (1976) pp. 1013-1020.

Ravitz L. "Bioelectric Correlates of Emotional States." Connecticut State Medical Journal 16 (1952) pp. 499-505.

Ravitz L. "Application of Electrodynamic Field Theory in Biology, Psychiatry, Medicine and Hypnosis I. General Survey." American Journal of Clinical Hypnosis 1 (1959) pp. 135-150.

Reed B., Hagan B. "The Increasing Respectability of the Aura." Medical Journal of Australia 198 (1981) pp. 611-612.

Rose R. "Endocrine Responses to Stressful Psychological Events." Psychiatric Clinics of North America 3 (1980) pp. 251-276.

Scheier M. "Optimism, Coping and Health: Assessment and Implications of Generalized Outcome Expectancies." Health Psychology 4 (1985) pp. 219-247.

Shaver P. and Friedman J. "Your Pursuit of Happiness." Psychology Today August 26, 1976, pp. 29.

Simonton O. and Simonton S. "Belief Systems and Management of Emotional Aspects of Malignancy." Journal of Transpersonal Psychology 7 (1975) pp. 29-47.

Smith J. "The Influence of Enzyme Growth by the Laying on of Hands" In *The Dimensions of Healing: A Symposium*. 1972, Los Altos, CA: The Academy of Parapsychology and Medicine.

Smith J. "Enzymes are Activated by the Laying-On of Hands." Human Dimensions 2 (1972) pp. 46-48.

Thomas C. and Duszynski D. "Closeness to Parents and the Family Constellation in a Prospective Study of Five Disease States: Suicide, Mental Illness, Malignant Tumors, Hypertension and Coronary Heart Disease." The Johns Hopkins Medical Journal 134 (1973) pp. 251-270.

Tiller W. "Some Energy Field Observations of Man and Nature." In *The Kirlian Aura*. (eds) Kripner and Rubin. 1974, Garden City, NY: Doubleday.

Tiller W. "Creating a New Functional Model of Body Healing Energies." Journal of Holistic Health 4 (1979) pp. 102-114.

Tiller W. "Energy Fields and the Human Body." (ed) J White. *Frontiers of Consciousness*. 1974, New York: Avon Books.

Wallace R. and Benson H. "The Physiology of Meditation." Scientific American 226 (1972) pp. 84-90.

Whitcher S. "Multidimensional Reaction to Therapeutic Touch in a Hospital Setting." Journal of Personality and Social Psychology 37 (1979) pp. 87-96.

Willis G. "The Reversibility of Atherosclerosis." Canadian Medical Journal 77 (1957) pp. 106.

Wolf S. "The Pharmacology of Placebos." Pharmacology 11 (1959) pp. 689-704.

Zajonc R. "Emotion and Facial Efference: A Theory Reclaimed." Science 228 (1985) pp. 1521.

Index

Give the Gift of Healing
to a Friend or Colleague

Yes, please send me _____ copies of *Healing, Health, and Transformation* at $19.95 each, plus $2 per book for shipping and handling. (Illinois residents please add $1.60 states sales tax.) Allow 30 days for delivery.

Name _____

Phone (___) _____

Address _____

City/State/Zip _____

$ ___ check/MO enclosed. Charge my □ VISA □ MC

Card Number _____ Expires _____

Signature _____

Mail to: Lavonne Press,
            P.O. Box 81709, Chicago IL 60681-0709.
Phone credit card orders to (800) 369-HEAL (4325)

FOR MORE INFORMATION

Dr. Ferguson is available for lectures, conferences, workshops, and speaking engagements throughout the country. She enjoys inspiring her audiences on topics of healing, love, health, and transformation.

If you are interested in responding to this book, please write:

Elaine R. Ferguson, M.D.
500 North Michigan Ave., Suite 1920
Chicago, IL 60681-0709